Baby
with the
Bathwater
Laughing
Wild

Baby with the Bathwater

AND

Laughing Wild

TWO PLAYS BY

Christopher Durang

 Grove Press

NEW YORK

Published by Grove Press
a division of Wheatland Corporation
841 Broadway
New York, N.Y. 10003

Library of Congress Cataloging-in-Publication Data
Durang, Christopher, 1949–
   [Laughing wild]
   Laughing wild ; and, Baby with the bathwater : two plays / by
Christopher Durang.
     p.   cm.
   ISBN 0-8021-3130-1 (pbk.)
   I. Title: Laughing wild. II. Title: Baby with the bathwater.
PS3554.U666L3   1988   88-13938
812'.54—dc19   CIP

Designed by Irving Perkins Associates

Manufactured in the United States of America

This book is printed on acid-free paper.

First Edition 1989

10 9 8 7 6 5 4 3 2 1

Contents

Baby with the Bathwater

Baby with the Bathwater was first presented off-Broadway on November 9, 1983, by Playwrights Horizons in New York City; Andre Bishop, artistic director; Paul Daniels, managing director. The production was directed by Jerry Zaks; sets designed by Loren Sherman; costumes designed by Rita Ryack; lighting designed by Jennifer Tipton; sound designed by Jonathan Vall. Production stage manager was Esther Cohen; stage manager was Diane Ward. The cast was as follows:

HELEN	Christine Estabrook
JOHN	W. H. Macy
NANNY/KATE/PRINCIPAL	Dana Ivey
CYNTHIA/ANGELA/MISS PRINGLE/SUSAN	Leslie Geraci
YOUNG MAN	Keith Reddin

In the subsequent run of the play, the role of Nanny/Kate/Principal was taken over by Kate McGregor-Stewart, then by Mary Louise Wilson, then by Cynthia Darlow. The understudies were Melodie Somers and William Kux. During the play's final week Ms. Somers played the part of Helen.

Baby with the Bathwater had its world premiere at the American Repertory Theatre in Cambridge, Massachusetts, on March 31, 1983, Robert Brustein, artistic director, Rob Orchard, managing director. The production was directed by Mark Linn-Baker; sets designed by Don Soule; costumes designed by Liz Perlman; lighting designed by Thom Palm; sound designed by Randolph Head. Production stage manager was John Grant-Phillips. The cast was as follows:

HELEN	Cherry Jones
JOHN	Tony Shalhoub
NANNY/KATE/PRINCIPAL	Marianne Owen
CYNTHIA/ANGELA/MISS PRINGLE/SUSAN	Karen MacDonald
YOUNG MAN	Stephen Rowe

Characters

HELEN, the mother
JOHN, the father
NANNY, the nanny
CYNTHIA
KATE
ANGELA
MRS. WILLOUGHBY, the principal
MISS PRINGLE, a teacher
YOUNG MAN
SUSAN

The parts of NANNY, KATE, *and* MRS. WILLOUGHBY *may be played by the same actress. The parts of* CYNTHIA, ANGELA, MISS PRINGLE, *and* SUSAN *may be played by the same actress.*

Act I

The home of JOHN *and* HELEN, *a couple in their late twenties or early thirties. They are standing over a bassinet.*

HELEN: Hello, baby. Hello.

JOHN: It looks just like me.

HELEN: Yes it does. Smaller.

JOHN: Well, yes.

HELEN: And it looks just like me. It has my hair.

JOHN: Yes it does.

HELEN (*slightly worried*): I wonder if it would have been better off having your hair?

JOHN (*reassuringly*): Your hair is lovely.

HELEN (*touched*): Thank you.

JOHN: You're welcome. (*They smile at one another warmly. Back to the bassinet.*) Hello, baby. Hello. Cooooo.

HELEN: Cooooooo. Cummmmm-quat. Cummmmm-quat!

JOHN: Hee haw. Hee haw. Daddy's little baked potato.

7

HELEN: Don't call the child a baked potato.

JOHN: It's a term of affection.

HELEN: It isn't. It's a *food*. No one wants to be called a baked potato.

JOHN: Well, it doesn't speak English.

HELEN: The various books say that you should presume your child *can* understand you. We don't want it to have problems in kindergarten or marriage because you called it a baked potato.

JOHN: It seems to me you're losing your sense of humor.

HELEN (*firmly*): I just don't want to make the child insane—that's all. Bringing up a child is a delicate thing.

JOHN: All right, you're not a baked potato, sweet pea. (*She looks at him in horror; he senses her look.*) And you're not a sweet pea either. You're a baby. Bay-bee. Bay-bee.

HELEN: I want a divorce.

JOHN: What?

HELEN: You heard me. I want a divorce.

JOHN: Are you crazy? You've read the statistics on children from broken homes. Do you want to do that to our child?

HELEN: I don't feel ready for marriage, I didn't when we got married, I should have said no.

JOHN: But we love each other.

HELEN: You have blond hair. I don't like men with blond

hair. I like men with dark hair, but I'm afraid of them.
I'm not afraid of you. I hate you.

JOHN: What? Is this postpartum depression?

HELEN: Don't talk about postpartum depression, you
know nothing about it. (*To baby:*) Men just don't understand things, do they, sweetie pie?

JOHN: If I can't call it a potato, you can't call it a pie.

HELEN: I didn't call it a pie.

JOHN: You did. You said sweetie pie.

HELEN: Sweetie pie is an expression, it isn't a pie. You
don't go into a restaurant and order sweetie pie.

JOHN: Why do you insist on winning every argument?

HELEN: If I'm right, I'm right. It has nothing to do with
winning. (*To baby:*) Men don't know how to argue.
That's why they always end up hitting people.

JOHN: I don't hit people.

HELEN: Boys and men hit one another constantly. They
attack one another on the street, they play football, they
wrestle on television, they rape one another in prison,
they rape women and children in back alleys. (*To baby:*)
Beware of men, darling. Be glad you're not ever going to
be a man.

JOHN: That's an awful thing to say. And is it a girl? I
thought it was a boy.

HELEN: We don't know what sex it is. It's too young. The
doctor said we could decide later.

JOHN: You don't decide later. Gender is a fact, it's not a
decision.

HELEN: That's not what the doctor said to me. He said something about the DNA molecule. They're splitting it differently now. He said if the DNA combined one way, the child would have testosterone and then we could either have it circumcised or not, depending. Or else the DNA combines with estrogen, in which case it would be a girl. Or in some cases, the DNA combines with cobalt molecules, and then the child would be radioactive for 5,000 years and we'd have to send it out into orbit.

JOHN: What are you talking about?

HELEN: Can't you speak English? I'm married to an idiot. (*To baby:*) Your father is an idiot. Oh God, please let me meet a dark-haired man who's smarter than I am. (*To* JOHN:) Oh why don't you go away? I don't like you.

JOHN: I don't understand. We were very happy yesterday.

HELEN: What are you talking about? Happy? Who was happy?

JOHN: We were. We were making plans. The child's schooling, what playground to take it to, whether to let it play with toy guns, how to toilet train it.

HELEN: Oh God, toilet training. I can't face it. We'll have to hire someone.

JOHN: We don't have money to hire anyone.

HELEN: Well, we'll have to earn the money.

JOHN: But we can't earn money. I was let go from work.

HELEN: Well, you can find another job.

JOHN: I need rest, I really don't feel able to work right now.

HELEN: John, that's not practical.

JOHN: I want to go back to bed.

HELEN: But, John, you wanted to be responsible, don't you remember? Right after that week you stayed behind the refrigerator, you came to me and said, "The immaturities of my youth are over now, Helen. Let's make a baby." And then we did. Don't you remember?

JOHN: I need professional help. I want to go to McLean in Massachusetts. That's the institution James Taylor was in for a time. He seems so tranquil and calm when he gives his concerts. And he has a summer house on Martha's Vineyard. Maybe, when the doctor says I'm well enough, I could go to Mar—

HELEN: JOHN, LIVE UP TO YOUR RESPONSI-BILITIES! (*Baby cries.*) Oh, God, it's crying. What should we do?

JOHN: Sing to it.

HELEN (*sings to baby sweetly, softly*): There's no business like show business, like no business . . .

JOHN: A lullaby, sweetheart.

HELEN: I don't know any lullabies.

JOHN (*sings*):
  Hush little baby, don't you cry,
  Mama's gonna give you a big black eye . . .

HELEN: Good heavens, those aren't the lyrics.

JOHN: I know they're not. I can't remember the right ones.

HELEN: Oh God. You're going to teach baby all the

wrong lyrics to everything. It's going to have trouble with its peer group.

JOHN: Maybe we should hold it to stop it crying.

HELEN: We might drop it. I had a cocktail for breakfast. I'm not steady.

JOHN: Why did you have a cocktail?

HELEN: You're always picking on me! I'm sorry I married you. I'm sorry I gave birth to baby. I wish I were back at the Spence School.

JOHN: We love the baby.

HELEN: How can we love the baby? It won't stop that noise. (*To baby:*) Shut up, baby. Shut up. Oh God, please help us. Please make the baby stop.

> (*Enter* NANNY, *dressed in tweeds, wearing a lady-like hat and carrying a large cloth handbag.*)

NANNY: Hello. I'm Nanny.

HELEN: Oh thank goodness you've come. Please make it stop crying.

NANNY (*goes over to crib; in a high, soothing, if odd, voice*): Helloooooooo, baby. Hellllloooooo. Yeeeeeeeees. Yeeeeeees. It's Nanny. Yesssssssssssss. (*Baby stops making noise.*) That's right. That's right. I've brought you a present.

> (*Takes out a jar; opens it—it's a trick jar—and a large snake pops out. Baby screams in terror.* JOHN *and* HELEN *are fairly startled also.* NANNY *laughs.*)

Ha haha haha! That surprised you, didn't it?

JOHN: See here, who are you?

HELEN: Oh my God, it's crying again. *Please* make it stop crying.

NANNY: What? I can't hear you. Child's making so much racket.

HELEN: Please. Make it stop that awful noise.

NANNY (*high voice again*): Quiet, little baby. Be quiet. (*No effect; then she yells stridently.*) SHUT UP! (*Baby is abruptly quiet;* NANNY *is pleased.*)

JOHN (*looking at the baby*): I think you've given it a heart attack.

NANNY: No, no, it's just resting.

HELEN: Oh thank goodness it stopped.

JOHN: Who are you?

NANNY: I am the ghost of Christmas Past. Hahahahaha. No—just making a joke. I get a list of all the new parents from the hospital, and then I just *descend* upon them. Now, I need Wednesday evenings off, and I'm allergic to asparagus and lobster . . .

HELEN: We never have lobster.

NANNY: And I like chunky peanut butter better than the smooth kind, but if you already have the smooth kind, we'll finish that off before you buy a new jar.

JOHN: I can't afford you.

NANNY: And I don't do windows, and I don't do floors, and I don't do laundry, but I make salmon salad and tuna salad and salad niçoise and chef salad and chunky peanut butter sandwiches, and I make my own yogurt in a great big vat.

JOHN: You can't stay here.

HELEN: But I need help. I can't cope by myself. Please, John.

JOHN: But I'm on unemployment.

NANNY: Well, we'll just get you another job.

JOHN: But what can I do?

NANNY: Why don't you become an astronaut? That pays very well. Or a football player. Or a newscaster. (*To baby:*) Wouldn't you like to see your daddy on television, baby? Baby? (*Looks into the silent bassinet.*) I think the snake scared it. (*To baby:*) WAKE UP! (*Baby cries.*) There, that's better. (*Smiles, pleased.*)

HELEN: Please don't shout at it. It's not good for it.

JOHN: Maybe I should hold it to comfort it.

HELEN: That would be very responsible, John. That's a good boy. Good boy.

JOHN: Thank you. (*Holds baby, who stops crying.*)

HELEN: John's been fired from his job, you see.

NANNY: Well, that won't put food on the table.

HELEN: I could get a job, I suppose. But what would I do?

NANNY: Well, why don't you write a novel? *The World According to Garp* sold very well recently. Why don't you write something like that?

HELEN: Oh, that's a good idea. But I need a pencil and paper.

NANNY: Oh. Well, here's a dollar. Now you go to the store and buy some paper and a nice felt-tip pen.

HELEN: Now?

NANNY: No time like the present. Right, baby?

HELEN: Oh, John, please put the baby down. I'm afraid one of us might drop it. (*To* NANNY:) I had a cocktail for breakfast, and John took some Nyquil and Quaaludes.

JOHN: I get tense.

NANNY: Put the baby down, John. You're spoiling it. (*Takes it from him, puts it in bassinet.*) Now, what should we call it, do you think?

HELEN: Well, John's father's name was John, and his mother's name was Joan, and my father's name was John, and my mother's name was Hillary, and my doctor's name is Dr. Arthur Hammerstein, but I really want a woman doctor who can understand me, but it's so hard to find a doctor.

NANNY: Yes, but what about a name, a name?

HELEN: Don't you get cross with me.

NANNY: All right, we won't call the baby anything.

JOHN: We could call it John after me if it's a boy, and Helen after you if it's a girl.

HELEN: No, I don't want to call it anything now. I'm going back to bed.

NANNY: I thought you were going to buy paper and pencil to start your novel.

HELEN: I don't want to. I want to sleep.

NANNY: I gave you a dollar.

HELEN: I don't care.

NANNY: Here's another dollar. Go buy yourself an ice cream soda on the way home.

HELEN: Oh, thank you Nanny. I love you. (*Hugs her, runs off.*)

NANNY: We're all going to have to be very kind to her. (*To baby:*) Don't depend on mommy, baby. She's not all there. (*To* JOHN:) So—what can I do for you?

JOHN: I really haven't hired you yet, you know.

NANNY: You want a quick one?

JOHN: Pardon?

NANNY: Us older girls have a few tricks up our sleeves, you know. I bet I know some things your wife doesn't know.

JOHN: I don't know. I had a Quaalude this morning, I don't really feel up to anything.

NANNY: It's very rude to turn me down. You might hurt my feelings.

JOHN: Well, what about the baby?

NANNY: The baby doesn't have to know anything about it. Now we haven't much time, she's getting the paper and pen and the ice cream soda.

JOHN: Well, all right, but let's not do it here. I feel uncomfortable in front of the baby.

NANNY: We could distract it. We could play loud music.

JOHN: But we might hurt its eardrums. I want to be a good father.

NANNY: Well, of course you do. I have tiny little earplugs we could put in its ears.

JOHN: Well, then, what's the point of the loud music?

NANNY (*thinks, but can't unravel the mystery*): I don't know.

JOHN: This is all getting too complicated.

NANNY (*cheerfully*): Very well! Let's just do it in the kitchen. Come on.

> (*She energetically drags* JOHN *off into the kitchen. After a moment, the baby starts to cry. A young woman, rather sweet looking but dressed shabbily, enters the apartment. Her name is* CYNTHIA. *She appears to have wandered into the apartment for no apparent reason. She is very pregnant. She walks over to the bassinet and sings sweetly to the baby to comfort it. After a few lines of the song, the baby does stop crying.* CYNTHIA *keeps singing to it for a while; her voice is pleasant and soothing.*)

CYNTHIA (*sings*):
> Hush, little baby,
> Don't say a word,
> Momma's gonna buy you a mockingbird,
> And if that mockingbird don't sing,
> Momma's gonna buy you a golden ring,
> And if that golden ring turns brass,
> Momma's gonna buy you a looking glass,
> And if that looking glass gets broke,
> Momma's gonna buy you a billy goat.

> (*Hums.* CYNTHIA *smiles that the baby has been comforted and, still humming, wanders back out of the apartment. Lights dim.*)

S C E N E 2

Later that night. Dark. Baby cries. Voices saying "Oh God." The lights come up. The couch has been opened up to make a bed. In the bed are HELEN, NANNY, *and* JOHN *in nightgowns and pajamas.* NANNY *is sound asleep.*

HELEN: Baby, we're sleeping. Now go back to sleep. John, you talk to it.

JOHN: Enough of this noise, little child. Daddy and Mommy are sleeping.

HELEN: Oh God it won't stop. Nanny, wake up. Nanny!

JOHN: Nanny! (*They poke her.*)

NANNY (*coming out of a dream*): Where am I? Help! Water to the right of me, water to the left of me. Ode to a Grecian urn. (*Lies back down.*)

HELEN: Nanny, baby's calling you.

NANNY: I'm sleepy.

HELEN: Nanny, you're the nanny.

NANNY (*pointing to* JOHN): What about Tiger here?

JOHN: Don't call me Tiger.

NANNY: Tiger. Ruff. Ruff. (*Gets up.*) All right, baby. Nanny's coming. (*Picks up baby.*) Helloooooooo, baby. Hellllooooooo, baby. That's right. Wheeeeeeeeeeeeee. Wooooooooooooooo. Waaaaaaaaaaaa. (*Keeps making these odd, if soothing, sounds softly through next dialogue. Baby does stop crying.*)

HELEN: Why did she call you Tiger?

JOHN: I don't know. She was probably dreaming.

HELEN: Oh, baby's stopped. Thank goodness for Nanny. And her salad niçoise was so good for dinner.

JOHN: Yes it was. Helen, I don't think this is going to work out.

HELEN: What isn't?

JOHN: Nanny.

HELEN: I think it's working out fine.

JOHN: I can't sleep three in a bed.

HELEN: John, when we're rich we'll buy a big house with an extra room for Nanny. Until then, this is fine.

JOHN: Helen, I don't think Nanny is a good person.

NANNY: I heard that.

JOHN: Nanny, please, we're trying to have a private conversation.

NANNY: Don't you talk behind my back. I'll hire a lawyer. We'll slap an injunction against you.

JOHN: Please, you deal with baby, and let Helen and me figure this out.

NANNY: I've finished comforting baby. (*Brusquely.*) Go to sleep, baby. (*Tosses it back into the bassinet.*) Now you say to my face that I'm not a good person.

JOHN: Well maybe that's too strong. But I think you're too rough with baby. I mean, you just threw it into the bassinet.

NANNY: Do you hear it crying?

JOHN: No, but maybe it's fainted or something.

NANNY: It's just resting.

JOHN: You keep saying that, but I think you have it fainting. And it has this look of panic on its face.

NANNY: Look, don't tell me how to handle children. I got it down.

HELEN: Nanny knows best, John. And she's helping me with my novel. She liked the first chapter, John.

NANNY: I did. I thought it showed real promise.

HELEN: And then when I sell my novel, if we get a good deal for the paperback rights, then we can buy a house in the country and maybe we can have another baby.

JOHN: Helen, Nanny seduced me this afternoon when you were out buying paper.

NANNY: That's a lie.

JOHN: It's the truth. I was unfaithful to you, Helen. (HELEN *looks hurt in earnest.*) I'm sorry.

HELEN: I don't know how to cope with this.

JOHN: So you can see why I don't feel comfortable all three of us in the bed.

HELEN (*near tears*): I don't know how to cope.

JOHN: I'm really sorry. It was Nanny's fault.

NANNY: He raped me!

JOHN: I didn't. That's a lie, Helen.

HELEN: I don't want to talk about this anymore! I'm

going to work on my novel in the kitchen, and I'm going to pretend that I live alone. (*Exits.*)

JOHN: Well, things are in a fine mess.

NANNY: You told her, I didn't.

JOHN: What we did was wrong.

NANNY: Oh for God's sake, it didn't mean anything. It would've been fine if you hadn't told her.

JOHN: I felt guilty. It's wrong to cheat on your wife.

NANNY: You're such a dullard. There is no right or wrong, there's only *fun!*

JOHN: That can't be true. I mean, there are certain things that are intrinsically wrong, and when we figure out what these things are, then we are said to have values.

NANNY: Haven't you read *The Brothers Karamazov?* Ivan Karamazov realizes that because there is no God, everything is permitted.

JOHN: I don't understand.

NANNY: Everything is permitted. (*Hits the back of his head hard.*)

JOHN: Why did you do that?

NANNY: I *felt* like it. Everything is permitted. (*Laughs.*)

> (*Re-enter* HELEN, *in raincoat and rain hat, holding a sheaf of papers.*)

HELEN: I'm taking my coat and the first chapter of my novel and the baby, and I'm leaving you.

JOHN: Helen, I'm sorry, it won't happen again.

HELEN: You obviously prefer Nanny to me, and so as far as I'm concerned, you can just go to hell.

NANNY (*genuinely meaning it*): Oh I love arguments.

JOHN: Helen, we have to stay together for the baby.

HELEN: No, I'm taking the baby and the novel, and you won't get any of the paperback rights at all. Goodbye.

JOHN: The baby's asleep.

HELEN: Or fainted, as you said, Nanny bats it around so. (*Picks up baby.*) Mommy's going to save you now, sweetie pie.

JOHN: I have rights to the baby too.

HELEN: Baby will thank me later.

JOHN: But where will you go at this hour?

HELEN (*at a loss*): We'll go to . . . Marriott's Essex House.

JOHN: Our credit cards have been cancelled.

HELEN: All right. We'll sleep in the park, I don't care, I just have to leave here! Don't touch me!

JOHN: But it's freezing out. Baby will catch pneumonia.

HELEN: Well I can't help it. You don't *die* from pneumonia.

JOHN: But you do, you do die from pneumonia!

HELEN: Don't tell me what to do. I KNOW WHAT I'M DOING! (*Exits with baby.*)

JOHN: Helen!

NANNY: Let her go, she'll be back in a few minutes. I know these hysterical mothers.

JOHN: They're going to get very ill, it's very cold outside.

NANNY: It's bad to fuss too much as a parent, your child will grow up afraid. Let baby discover some things for itself. You want a quick one?

JOHN: What?

NANNY: You heard me.

JOHN: But it's wrong. Sexual infidelity is *wrong*.

NANNY: Wrong, right, I don't know where you pick up these phrases. Didn't they teach you about Darwin in public school? The fish came out of the water, covered with a viscous substance, and then bones and vertebrae were evolved, and then male and female, and then the egg and the ovum and the testicles and the semen, and then reproduction, and then dinosaurs, or maybe dinosaurs before that, and then local governments, and then the space program, and then nuclear power plants and now cable television and Home Box Office. *Where* do you find right and wrong in all that??? Tell me.

(*Re-enter* HELEN, *wet, with baby, wet.*)

HELEN: I fell in a puddle. I'm all wet.

NANNY: Well, if it isn't Nora five minutes after the end of *A Doll's House.*

HELEN: I thought you were going to help me, and now all you do is pick on me.

JOHN: Good God, the baby's soaking wet.

HELEN: Of course, it's wet. I told you I fell in a puddle.

NANNY: Helen is the worst mother, isn't she, baby?

HELEN: Don't you say that. John, hit her for me.

JOHN (*suddenly very forceful*): Now enough of all this arguing! We're going to get baby in some dry clothes, and Helen in some dry clothes, and then we're going to take Nyquil and Quaaludes and get some sleep! And we will discuss all these problems in the morning. Is that clear?

HELEN: Yes, John.

NANNY: Yes, John.

JOHN: Very well. Now no more talking.

> (JOHN *puts baby in bassinet and changes its clothes;* HELEN *starts to take off her things, sneezing occasionally.* NANNY *exits, re-enters.*)

NANNY: I've got the Nyquil.

JOHN: Thank God.

NANNY: You have its feet in the armholes.

JOHN: The point is that it's dry, right?

NANNY: The point is to do things right.

HELEN: You said no more talking. I want to go to sleep.

JOHN: All right. But in the morning, we're going to kill Nanny.

> (NANNY *looks at* JOHN *with suspicion.*)

HELEN: Let's just have our Nyquil and not argue anymore.

JOHN: Should we give baby Nyquil?

HELEN: Oh I don't know. What does it say on the label?

JOHN: I don't know. I can't read the small print. I need glasses.

HELEN: Well if you can't read, then there's no solution, is there?

NANNY: Why don't we just ask baby? Do you want some Nyquil, honey? Do you? Huh? (*Pause.*) It won't say. It's just staring back, hostilely.

HELEN: Oh why can't it be a happy baby? (*Notices its clothing.*) John, you've dressed it all wrong. It can barely move that way.

JOHN: I'm going to sleep now. I don't want to hear any more complaints! (JOHN, HELEN, *and* NANNY *get into bed.*)

NANNY: Good night everybody.

HELEN: Good night, Nanny. (*Kisses her.*) I love you. (*To* JOHN:) I hate you.

JOHN: Good night, Helen.

>(*They lie down to sleep. After a moment* CYNTHIA *enters. She goes to the bassinet.*)

CYNTHIA: Hello, baby. Helllooooooo.

>(*The three in bed sit up and stare at her.*)

HELEN: Who are you?

CYNTHIA: I'm just so upset. I'm very poor, and I gave birth in the hospital to a darling little boy, or girl, and when I came home from the hospital, there's no heat in my apartment and there's no furniture, there's just my German shepherd. And, of course, I hadn't fed it in about a week, since I went into the hospital, so I went out to buy some baby food and some dog food. But there's no furniture, so I left the baby on the floor, and when I came back, the dog had eaten the baby. And now I don't know what to do.

NANNY: Have you told this story to the *New York Post*?

CYNTHIA: No.

NANNY: Well, I'd start out by doing that.

CYNTHIA: But I'm so tired now.

JOHN: What is the matter with you? Why did you leave your baby on the floor?

CYNTHIA: Please don't yell at me. I don't have any furniture!

NANNY: There, there, you poor thing. We'll get you another baby. You'll adopt.

CYNTHIA: But I'm not a fit mother.

NANNY: Everyone's allowed one mistake.

HELEN (*suspiciously*): Where's the dog?

CYNTHIA: I have it right outside in the hallway. Would you like to keep it?

(*She goes to the door;* JOHN *springs up and blocks the door.*)

JOHN: Don't you bring that dog in here!

NANNY: Now there's no reason to hold this woman's

stupidity against her dog. That's unfair. (*To* CYNTHIA:) Of course, we want the dog. It sounds like a good watch-dog.

CYNTHIA: Well actually it's always been vicious, but you see normally I feed it. It's just that when I was in the hospital, they wouldn't let me leave.

NANNY: Administrative red tape. It's really behind so much evil and suffering in the world.

HELEN: I don't know. I think she's a terrible woman.

CYNTHIA: Oh, please, I feel so guilty. Don't hate me. I really just don't know any better. I didn't listen to anything they taught me in school. Something about equal sides of an isosceles triangle. And I don't have any furniture at home. And you have lovely furniture. Do you mind if I lie down and sleep for a moment? I'm really exhausted. (*She lies down on the sofa bed and falls asleep immediately.*)

NANNY: Poor child.

HELEN: Why is she here? We don't want her here.

NANNY: Where is your charity? The poor child is going to have to live with her stupidity all the rest of her life. Maybe she'll even have to go to prison when the police hear of it all. Surely you wouldn't begrudge her one night's sleep of safety and peace?

HELEN: Well, maybe not. But can we make her go in the morning?

NANNY: We'll see. Come, John, come to bed. Tomorrow's going to be a busy day. (NANNY, HELEN, *and* JOHN *lie down next to the sleeping* CYNTHIA. *Lights dim.*)

S C E N E 3

*Sound of dog barking viciously; baby crying.
Lights up on the four of them in the sofa bed.*

HELEN: Someone make that noise stop.

JOHN: Be quiet, baby.

HELEN: Is baby barking?

JOHN: Oh God, that dog. (*To* CYNTHIA:) Hey, you, wake up. Shut up your dog somehow.

CYNTHIA: I was having such a pleasant dream.

JOHN: Make your dog be quiet.

CYNTHIA: What dog?

JOHN: Your dog is barking.

CYNTHIA (*pleasantly*): Oh yes, I hear it now. It must smell baby.

HELEN: Oh dear God.

CYNTHIA: Don't be alarmed. It's just hungry. Do you have any red meat?

JOHN: Maybe there's some red meat in the refrigerator.

CYNTHIA: Well go give it some, and then it'll stop barking. (*Smiles.*) Don't let it get your hand though.

(JOHN *exits to kitchen.*)

HELEN: Where did you get the dog?

CYNTHIA: Oh, some terrible people were beating it in the park, and I felt sorry for it, so I asked them if I could have it.

HELEN: And so they gave it to you?

CYNTHIA: Yes. They beat me up for quite a while. Twenty minutes, it seemed, maybe it was shorter, it's hard to judge time that way. And then the dog and I crawled to my apartment, and we've just been together ever since.

> (JOHN *returns from the kitchen with package of chopped meat, goes into the hall to the barking dog. Barking gets worse, then ferocious eating noises occur.* JOHN *comes back.*)

JOHN: It took the meat.

CYNTHIA: It really *loves* meat. I'm a vegetarian myself. I tried to make the dog eat bean sprouts and broccoli once for a while, but it didn't work out.

JOHN: Someone should really change baby. I think it's made a mess.

HELEN: Oh, I don't want to. Let Nanny do it.

NANNY (*not moving*): I'm sleeping.

CYNTHIA: Oh, I'll do it. I love babies. (*Goes to baby.*) I had the most wonderful dream last night. I dreamt that I kidnapped your baby, and that the dog, baby, and myself took a bus to Florida and had a wonderful time on the beach. (*On the word "kidnapped," the three in bed sit up and look at her with varying degrees of concern.*) I'm afraid we all got seriously sunburned in the dream, but I don't know if we died from it or not because then I woke up with the dog barking. Oh, your baby's so grumpy looking. What's the matter, baby? Don't you like me?

HELEN: It's a very grouchy baby. We're not very happy with it.

CYNTHIA: I know. I have a little toy it will like. The nurses gave it to me at the hospital. (*Holds up little red toy that jingles when she shakes it.*) Hey? It's a little red thingamajig. Isn't it cute? I don't think baby likes me. Why don't you like me, baby?

NANNY (*with great disinterest*): Why don't you read to it then? Baby loves to be read to. (*Exits to get into her nanny clothes.*)

CYNTHIA: Oh all right. (*Meanders about, looking for a book.*)

HELEN: John, you better get up and go look for work.

JOHN: I just want to sleep. Leave me alone. (*Hides under pillow.*)

HELEN: John, you have responsibilities. Look at me.

CYNTHIA: Here's a book. Now, if I read to you, will you promise to smile at me, baby?

JOHN: Let's get a divorce. You wanted one yesterday. Let's get one now.

HELEN: It's not practical now. Baby needs a father, and I need financial support until I finish my novel.

CYNTHIA: Chapter seven. "Shortly after Mommie Dearest won her Oscar for *Mildred Pierce*, she would burst

into Christopher's and my room at three in the morning
screaming, 'Fire drill! Fire drill!' "

(JOHN *and* HELEN *look at* CYNTHIA *for a moment,
then return to their argument.*)

JOHN: Helen, this novel idea is a pipe dream. Don't you
know that?

HELEN: It is not. Nanny said my first chapter was brilliant.

NANNY (*offstage*): Well, not brilliant perhaps. But quite
commercial, I'd say.

CYNTHIA: "Then she'd pour gasoline on the curtains and
set them on fire, while we'd scream and scream."
(*Makes playful scream noises.*) Aaaaggh! Aaaaggh!

JOHN: But you can't write, don't you know that?

HELEN: What do you know? I can too! (NANNY *re-enters
with Helen's still soggy sheaf of papers.*)

NANNY: Read him your first chapter then, that'll
show him.

CYNTHIA: "I would try to untie Christopher from his
bed, but Mommie wouldn't let me."

HELEN (*proudly*): Chapter one. "I am born. I was born in
a workhouse in London in 1853."

(CYNTHIA *returns to reading to the baby as* HELEN
continues to read from her novel. NANNY *and*
JOHN *do their best to give* HELEN *their attention,
but find their focus hopelessly caught between
the two novel readings. Eventually* JOHN *and*
NANNY *begin to look discouraged and disoriented by how difficult it is to follow either story.*)

HELEN: "My mother, who-ever she may have been, had left me at the doorstep of a wealthy man named Mr. Squire of Squireford Manor. However, wicked traveling gypsies came by the squire's doorstep and snatched me up and left me at the workhouse. My first conscious memory is of little Nell, the cobbler's daughter, being run over by a coach and four."

CYNTHIA: "As the burning curtains came closer and closer to Christopher's bed, he cried aloud, 'God in heaven, save me from Mommie!' Then Mommie took out a fire extin-guisher and sprayed the curtains as well as Chris-topher and myself. And then with tears streaming down her cheeks, Mom-mie screamed, 'Clean up your rooms! Bad Chris-tina! Bad Christopher! Look at this dirt!' "

HELEN (*unable to stand it anymore*): WILL YOU BE QUIET???? I am *trying* to read from my novel.

CYNTHIA: I am reading to baby.

HELEN: I don't care what you're doing. You're a guest in this house.

CYNTHIA: Baby will grow up with no love of literature if you don't read to it.

HELEN: It's my baby, and I'll raise it as I see fit.

CYNTHIA: No, it's my baby! (*Snatches it up.*) I can see that my dream was a sign I should have it!

HELEN: Give it back to me at once!

CYNTHIA: No, I won't! You're not fit parents. I know I'm guilty of negligence with my baby, but it was an honest mistake. And I love babies. But you three are heartless. You don't hold the baby when it cries, you dress it wrong so it can't move in its pajamas, and you're both so inconsistent as people, changing from one mood to another, that you'll obviously make it crazy. That's why it never smiles. I may be forgetful, but baby has a chance with me!

HELEN: Give it back to me! (*Runs toward her.*)

CYNTHIA: Don't come near me, or I'll throw it out the window!

JOHN: Good Lord, she's insane.

> (*Everyone stands very still.* CYNTHIA *starts to move slowly to the door.*)

CYNTHIA: Now I'm going to leave here with baby and with the dog, and we're going to go to Florida, and you're not to follow us.

NANNY: Now let the dream be a warning. Don't stay in the sun too long. Babies have light skin.

CYNTHIA: I know what I'm doing. Come on, baby, you'll be safe with me. (*Runs out door, dog barks.*) Come on, doggie, it's just me and baby. (*Sound of dog barking, baby crying.*)

HELEN: John, what should we do?

NANNY: You could have another baby.

HELEN: John, we have to go after her.

JOHN: I need amphetamines.

HELEN: John, we haven't time.

JOHN: I told you we shouldn't have let her stay here.

HELEN: You said no such thing. And that's not the point now anyway. We've got to run after her.

JOHN: We're not dressed.

HELEN: Oh you're impossible. (*She runs out.*)

JOHN: You're right. I'm coming. (*He runs out too.*)

NANNY (*to audience, friendly*): Well, time to move on here, I think. I've done all I can do here. So I'll just pack. (*Notices something.*) Oh, she forgot her little red toy. Oh, too bad. (*Picks toy up, reads something on it.*) "Caution. Keep away from children. Contains lead, asbestos, and red dye number two." (*Laughs.*) Well, I guess it isn't meant as a child's toy at all then. (*Looks at it with utter bafflement.*) But what would it be meant as, I wonder? (*Energized by an idea.*) Maybe it *is* a toy, and the cautionary warning is *satiric!* (*Tosses the toy into bassinet.*) Hard to tell. So many mysteries. But children can survive it all, they are sturdy creatures. They ebb and flow, children do; they have great resiliency. (*Warmly.*) They abide and they endure.

> (*Re-enter* JOHN *and* HELEN, *holding baby. They are giddy with relief.*)

JOHN: We got it.

NANNY: Oh, did you?

HELEN: Yes, the stupid girl ran right in front of a bus, it ran right over her.

JOHN: Squashed her.

HELEN: Baby was just lucky and fell between the wheels.

NANNY: Oh that was lucky. Children are sturdy creatures, they ebb and flow.

HELEN: The dog was still living, so John pushed it in front of an oncoming car, and now it's dead too.

JOHN: The motorist was *real* angry. But it seemed too complicated to explain, so we just grabbed baby and ran.

HELEN: Thank goodness. (*Looks at baby.*) Baby looks so startled. It's been a busy day, hasn't it? Yessss.

JOHN: Nanny, Helen and I were talking while we ran back here, and things are going to be different now. The immaturities of my youth are over and I'm going to take the responsibility of being a father, and Helen is going to be a mother. And we're not letting any more crackpots into our home.

HELEN: That's right, John.

JOHN: And so, Nanny, I'm going to have to ask you to leave now. Helen and I have both decided that you're insane.

NANNY (*crosses to them*): When it cries, you hold it. You should feed it regularly. You should keep it clean. Be consistent with it. Don't coo one minute and shout the next.

HELEN: I'm giving up my career as a novelist to care for baby. And any resentment I feel I won't ever show.

NANNY: Well that all sounds excellent. Goodbye, Helen. Goodbye, Tiger.

HELEN: Goodbye, Nanny. We love you.

JOHN: Goodbye.

(NANNY *smiles fondly and waves. Then exits.*)

HELEN (*after a moment*): Oh, John. I feel so lonely now.

JOHN: We have each other. And baby.

HELEN: That's true. I wish I didn't have a baby and that I had written *Scruples* instead.

JOHN: Well, I wish I were in McLean, but I thought we were going to be positive about things from now on.

HELEN: You're right. I was just kidding. Let's be parents now. Hellooo, baby. (*They put baby back into bassinet.*)

JOHN (*to baby*): Helllooo. Baby looks so startled.

HELEN: Well, of course, it's been a terrifying day. Baby had never even seen a bus before, let alone been under one. (*Lovingly, to the baby:*) Don't worry, sweetie pie. Mommy'll protect you from now on. She'll protect you from buses, and from dogs, and from crazy people, and from everything and anything that goes bump in the night.

JOHN (*playfully*): Bump, bump, bump.

HELEN (*fondly*): That's right, John.

JOHN: And Daddy loves you too, my little baked potato.

HELEN (*suddenly absolutely furious*): I TOLD YOU NOT TO CALL IT A BAKED POTATO!!!

JOHN: I'm sorry, I'm sorry. Jesus. You mustn't raise your voice that way around baby. You'll make it deaf or something.

HELEN: I'm sorry. I feel better now.

JOHN: Okay, we'll forget it. (*To baby:*) All over, baby. You're safe now, my little bak— Baby. No more shouting. Everything's fine. Can you smile for Daddy?

HELEN: Or Mommy?

JOHN: Can you smile for Mommy and Daddy? Here's a nice little red toy. (*Holds up the red toy.*) Won't that make you smile? Huh? Oh why won't it smile? SMILE, damn it, SMILE!

HELEN: Smile, baby!

BOTH (*angry*): SMILE! SMILE! SMILE! SMILE!

HELEN (*pleased*): Oh, John, look, it's smiling.

JOHN: That's right, baby.

HELEN: Do you think it's just pretending to smile to humor us?

JOHN: I think it's too young to be that complicated.

HELEN: Yes, but why would it smile at us when we shouted at it?

JOHN: I don't know. Maybe it's insane.

HELEN: I wonder which it is. Insane, or humoring us?

JOHN: Look, it's still smiling. Maybe it likes the toy. Do you like the toy, baby? Here, you play with it a while, baby. It makes a funny noise, doesn't it? Tingle tangle. Tingle tangle. (*The baby throws the toy out of the bassinet.*) Oh, it doesn't like the toy.

HELEN: What a fussy baby. (*Playfully.*) Fussy baby. Fussy baby.

JOHN (*happy*): Oh, it's still smiling.

HELEN: Fussy baby.

JOHN: Fussy wussy wussy.

BOTH (*fondly*): Fussy wussy wussy baby. Fussy wussy wussy baby. (*Lights dim.*)

Act II

SCENE 1

A park bench. Three women in park playground. The sounds of children playing. On the bench are: HELEN, *the mother from the previous scenes; she is looking straight ahead, smoking a cigarette, and seems unhappy, hostile. Next to her, and presently not paying attention to her, are* ANGELA, *a sweet, drably dressed woman, and* KATE, *a bright, sharp-tongued woman with a scarf tied around her head.* ANGELA *and* KATE *are looking straight ahead, watching their children, who are placed (in their and our imaginations) out in the audience.* KATE *is knitting.*

KATE: Be careful, Billy!

ANGELA: That's your son?

KATE: Yes. Billy. He has my eyes and mouth, and his father's nose.

ANGELA (*looking; squinting*): Yes, I can see that. Of course, I've never seen your husband's nose, but he does have your mouth and eyes.

KATE: Don't hang upside down, Billy! You'll crack your head open. (*To* ANGELA:) He's reckless, just like his uncle Fred.

39

ANGELA: Oh. Is that his favorite uncle?

KATE: No. He's never met Fred. Fred is dead. Is that your little girl?

ANGELA: Yes. Susie. Watch your head, Susie! It's such a full-time job looking after children.

KATE: Yes it is. Susie's a pretty child. (*Stares at* ANGELA *suspiciously.*) Is her father very handsome?

ANGELA: Yes. His whole family is very nice looking.

KATE: Oh that's nice. Nobody in our family is particularly good looking. Except for Fred, sort of, though you'd never know it from the way he ended up, all squashed that way.

ANGELA: How did he die?

KATE: Part of the roller skating craze. He didn't know how, and he skated right under a crosstown bus. (*Calls out.*) Be careful, Billy! (*Back to conversation.*) I don't think there's such a thing as a homely child, do you? I mean Billy may well grow up to be *quite* homely, but right now he's really very cute. And your daughter is downright pretty.

ANGELA: Thank you. (*Calls.*) Be careful of your face, Susie. Don't fall down on it.

HELEN: I have a child too, you know.

KATE: What?

HELEN: No one has asked me about my child.

KATE: Well, no one was talking to you.

HELEN: Well, I'm a human being. I deserve courtesy.

KATE: Where is your child?

HELEN: That's her lying on the ground. (*Calls.*) Get up, Daisy! Stop acting like a lump.

KATE: What's the matter with her?

HELEN: She's very depressed. She falls asleep all the time. You put her in the bathtub, she falls asleep. You put her on the toilet, she falls asleep. She's a depressing child. Get up, Daisy! Maybe one of the boys would poke her for me.

ANGELA: Maybe she has narcolepsy.

HELEN: You get that from a venereal disease, don't you? You're trying to say something nasty about me, aren't you?

ANGELA: Narcolepsy is a disease. Where people fall asleep. You should take your daughter to a doctor.

HELEN: All diseases are psychological. I'm not going to waste money on some dumb doctor who can't do anything about anything. She sleeps because she doesn't want to be awake. She has no joie de vivre. GET UP, DAISY! Hey, you, boy, the one with the stick . . . can you get my daughter up?

KATE (*staring; after a bit*): Billy, don't put the stick there, that's nasty.

ANGELA: Why isn't she moving?

HELEN: She's willful. GET UP YOU LUMP OF CLAY! (*To boy:*) Tug her hair a little.

KATE: Billy, leave the little girl alone and go play on the jungle gym. (*To* HELEN:) I don't want you encouraging my son to pick on women. That's not a very good thing to teach.

ANGELA: She still hasn't moved. Maybe she's fainted.

HELEN: She just does this to annoy me. It's very successful. (*Calls.*) YOU'RE VERY SUCCESSFUL, DAISY. YOU'RE GETTING THROUGH. (*Back to them.*) It's passive aggression. I do it with my husband. He says to me, did you make dinner, I lie down on the rug and don't move. He says, get up; I don't move a muscle. He gets on top of me and starts to screw me, I pretend it isn't happening. She gets it from me. (*Yells.*) DO AS I SAY NOT AS I DO, DAISY, I'VE TOLD YOU THAT!

KATE: That's no way to bring up a child.

HELEN: What do you know? Do you want a fat lip? Don't cross me, I could do something terrible to your child.

KATE: What did you say?

HELEN (*suddenly coy and girlish*): Oh nothing. My bark's worse than my bite. (*Calls viciously.*) Get up, Daisy! (*Sings, to* DAISY, *rather sweetly.*)
Daisy, Daisy,
Give me your answer, do,
I'm half crazy,
All for the love of you . . .

(*Hostile, to* KATE *and* ANGELA:) Sing. (*They hesitate.*) SING!

ALL THREE (KATE *and* ANGELA, *uncomfortable*):
It won't be a stylish marriage,
I can't afford a carriage,   HELEN (*echoing*):
But you'll look sweet . . .   Sweet.
Upon the seat . . .   Seat.
Of a bicycle built for two.

HELEN: Did she move?

ANGELA: I think her arm twitched a little.

HELEN: Oh, I bet she heard it. She loves that song. Don't you, Daisy? Well, I have to go home now. (*Sweetly.*) Goodbye. (*Calls out to* DAISY.) Get up, Daisy, we're going home, Mother can't stand the park another minute. Get up! (*Getting wild.*) Get up, damn you, get up! All right, Daisy, I'll give you till five and then I'm gonna step on your back. You listening? One ... two ... three ...

ANGELA: Get up, Daisy.

HELEN: ... four ... four and a half ... four and three-quarters ... Oh, look, there she goes.

KATE: My God, she's running *fast.*

(*They turn their heads in unison quickly, watching* DAISY *run out of sight.*)

HELEN: She's like that. Very inconsistent. One minute catatonic, the next minute she *moves* like a comet.

ANGELA: My God, she's running right toward that bus!

HELEN: Yes, she's always been drawn to buses. She's always running right out in front of them. Usually the driver stops in time.

KATE: My God, it's going to hit her!

HELEN: Well, it'll probably be fine.

(KATE *and* ANGELA *watch horrified, then there's a shriek of brakes, and they relax, horrified but relieved.*)

KATE: Thank God.

ANGELA: It came so close.

HELEN: This happens all the time. I get quite used to it. (*Suddenly switches to real maternal feelings, gets very upset.*) Oh my God, Daisy. Oh my God, she was almost killed. Oh God. Oh God. (*Weeps.*) Daisy, I'm coming, darling, don't move, honey, Mommy's coming. (*Runs off, very upset.*)

KATE: Good grief.

ANGELA: Well, at least the child's safe.

KATE: Do you think we should do something?

ANGELA: What do you mean?

KATE: I don't know. Contact social welfare or something.

ANGELA: I don't know. Maybe it's not her child. Maybe she's only baby-sitting.

KATE: I don't think so.

ANGELA: I don't think we should get involved.

KATE: All right, we won't do anything about her. We'll wait until we read about the child *dead* in the newspaper.

ANGELA: I read about that child they found dismembered in the garbage cans outside the Twenty-one Club. CBS is going to make a TV movie about it.

KATE: I don't think television should exploit the sufferings of real people like that.

ANGELA: But they've got all those hours of programming to do. They've got to fill it up with something.

KATE: I suppose.

ANGELA: I wouldn't like to be a television executive. You'd have to have ideas all the time, and then after a while if people don't like your ideas, they fire you.

KATE: This is really off the point of what we should do about that poor child.

ANGELA: I don't like to think about it.

KATE: Well, that won't help the child.

ANGELA: I don't like to concentrate on one thing for too long a period of time. It makes my brain hurt.

KATE: I don't think either the mother or the child are mentally well.

ANGELA: No, they're probably not, but who is nowadays? Everything's so outside our control. Chemical explosions in Elizabeth, New Jersey. Somebody killed Karen Silkwood. There are all these maniacs stalking Dolly Parton, the poor woman doesn't feel like *singing* anymore. John Hinckley, David Berkowitz, Ronald Reagan. It's so difficult to maintain joie de vivre in the face of such universal discouragement. (*Looks glum for a moment.*) I have to take a mood elevator. (*Takes a pill.*) I have this pharmacist friend, he gives me all sorts of things. I should be cheerful in a few minutes. (*Waits for pill to take effect.*)

KATE (*edging away*): Well, fine. We'll do nothing then. I'll look forward to the CBS movie about the child under the bus. (*Calls.*) Come on, Billy, we're going home. *Billy!* Don't put the stick there, that's rude. Leave Susie alone. (*Shocked.*) Billy! Don't put *that* there either, that's *very* rude. Now put that back. (*To* ANGELA:) I'm sorry. He's just that age now.

ANGELA: Oh that's all right. He probably meant it affectionately. I always think sex and affection are somehow connected, don't you?

KATE: Well, no, not really.

ANGELA: Oh, I do. People need affection, you know. Susie, come give mommy a hug. (*Lights dim.*)

S C E N E 2

Back in the home of HELEN *and* JOHN. *The room, though, is filled with many toys, some of them broken. There is also a pile of what seems to be laundry in clear audience view. Two little legs with red sneakers are partially visible, sticking out of the laundry pile.* JOHN *and* HELEN *are talking.*

JOHN: Well, I'm very upset. That's all I can say.

HELEN: I know. You've said that, you've said that. Get on with it.

JOHN: I mean, I just don't think we're good parents.

HELEN: Why do you say that? Did the bus run over the child? No. Did a bus run over her last week? No.

JOHN: Why does she keep running to buses? What's the matter with her?

HELEN: Nothing is the matter with her. She's just depressed. We have to cheer her up. (*Crosses to pile of laundry, speaks to it.*) Cheer up, Daisy! You're depressing us.

JOHN: And why does she lie in this pile of laundry all the time? Do you think that's normal?

HELEN: Daisy is just going through a phase. She thinks she's an inanimate object. She thinks she's a baked potato because of what you said to her when she was a baby. (*To pile of laundry:*) You're not a baked potato, sweet pea. You're Mommy's little darling. Mommy loves you. Mommy doesn't mind that she's not a novelist or that she's stayed in a bad marriage just for your sake. She's willing to make that sacrifice. (*Stares at laundry.*) Uh, you see how unresponsive she is. It's enough to make you want to shake and bake her.

JOHN: Helen, we can't talk about the child that way. Did you hear what you just said?

HELEN: I was making a point, John. I'm not talking about actually cooking her. You have no sense of irony. (*To* DAISY:) We're not going to eat you, Daisy. Mommy was speaking figuratively.

JOHN: Speaking of shake and bake, have you made dinner yet?

HELEN: Have I made *dinner* yet? (*Very nasty, utterly furious.*) Well, now, let me see. I can't remember. You were at unemployment, and then I was at the playground, and then Daisy tried to run in front of a bus— now I remember all these events . . . but as to dinner. I'm going to have to lie down and think. (*She lies down on the floor and won't move.*)

JOHN: Helen, don't do this again. You know it makes me

furious. Helen, stop staring at the ceiling. Helen! HELEN! (*Stares, has quick fit.*) GODDAMN IT! (*Takes one of Daisy's toys, smashes it.*) I've smashed one of Daisy's toys, Helen, do you want me to smash another one? Helen, get up! Look at me. All right, Helen, I'm going to smash another one of her toys . . . (*Hears himself.*) Good God, listen to me. What's happened to us? Helen, we're ruining that poor child. I'm going to take her and leave you. We've got to get away from you. (*Goes to pile of laundry.*) Get up, Daisy, Daddy loves you. Daisy, get up. (*Sings sweetly.*) Daisy, Daisy . . . GOD-DAMN IT, GET UP! (*Starts to tie laundry and* DAISY *into a manageable bundle.*) Okay, Daisy, I'll just have to carry you. Helen, I'm taking Daisy and the laundry and we're leaving you. (*Slings laundry over his shoulder.*) I don't know where we're going, but we've got to get away. Helen, can you hear me? Helen, we're leaving you. Goodbye.

HELEN (*sits up*): And you'll never get any of the paperback rights! (*Lies down again.*)

JOHN: There aren't any paperback rights, Helen! You live in a fool's paradise. We're leaving now. (*Starts to leave.*) I don't know where we're going, but we're going somewhere. (*Stops.*) I just need a drink first, though. Where's the vodka, Helen? Helen? (*Puts laundry down.*) Daisy, do you know where the vodka is? Daisy? Helen? Daisy? Helen? GODDAMN IT, I'M TALKING TO YOU PEOPLE, ARE YOU DEAF? (*Sits on floor.*) Oh God, how did I get in this position? Where is the vodka?

HELEN (*sits up*): It's in the toy duck. (*Does speech exercise.*) Toy duck, toy duck, toy duck. (*Lies down again.*)

JOHN: Oh right. Thank you. (*Goes to toy duck, reaches into it, takes out bottle of vodka.*) Why can't we have a liquor cabinet like normal people? (*Takes a couple of big swallows from the bottle of vodka.*) Want some, Helen? (*No response.*) Daisy? Daisy? (*Bitter.*) She's not a baked potato, she's a twenty per cent cotton, eighty per cent polyester pile of . . . (*at a loss*) pooka-poo.

HELEN (*sits up*): Pooka-poo, pooka-poo. Toy duck. Toy duck. Polly wolly windbag! Polly wolly windbag! Mee, mae, mah, moh, moo. Mee, mae, mah, moh, moo.

JOHN: Oh, Helen, you're talking again. I'm sorry I asked you about dinner. Want a cocktail?

HELEN: Thanks, I'm too tired. (*Lies down.*)

JOHN (*sings*):
    Daisy, Daisy, give me your answer, do . . .

    (*Finishes song, then begins another.*)
    Hush, little baby, don't you cry,
    Mama's gonna give you a big black eye . . .

HELEN (*lying down, but calm*): John, those aren't the lyrics.

JOHN: I know. I just don't know the lyrics. (*Sings.*)

    And if that big black eye turns purple . . .
    Mama's gonna give you a . . .
    (*Spoken.*) What rhymes with purple?

HELEN (*sits up*): I don't know. I'm not a rhyming dictionary. Ask Daisy.

JOHN: Daisy, honey, what rhymes with purple? Daisy? Daisy, what rhymes with purple? Daisy? (*Listens, apparently hears an answer.*) She says she doesn't know.

HELEN (*slightly hopeful*): Well at least she spoke today. That's *something*.

JOHN (*cheered*): Yes, that is something. (*Drinks. Lights fade.*)

S C E N E 3

A desk and chair. The PRINCIPAL *is seated. She is dressed handsomely, but looks somewhat severe.*

PRINCIPAL (*into intercom*): You can send Miss Pringle in now, Henry.

(*Enter* MISS PRINGLE, *a sympathetic looking teacher.*)

I love having a male secretary. It makes it all worthwhile. (*Into intercom:*) Sharpen all the pencils please, Henry. Then check the coffee pot. Hello, Miss Pringle, how are you?

MISS PRINGLE: I'm fine, Mrs. Willoughby, but I wanted to talk to you about Daisy Dingleberry.

PRINCIPAL: Oh yes, that peculiar child who's doing so well on the track team.

MISS PRINGLE: Yes, she runs very quickly, but I felt I should—

PRINCIPAL: Wait a moment, would you? (*Into intercom:*) Oh, Henry, check if we have enough nondairy creamer for the coffee, would you? Then I want you to go out and buy my husband a birthday present for me, I don't have time. Thank you, sweetie. (*Back to* Miss Pringle.) Now, I'm sorry, what were you saying?

Miss Pringle: Well, I'm worried about Daisy. She's doing very well in track, and some days she does well in her classes, and then some days she just stares, and then she's absent a lot.

Principal: Yes. Uh huh. Uh huh. Yes, I see. Uh huh. Uh huh. Go on.

Miss Pringle: Well, it's her summer essay, you know . . . "What I Did Last Summer"?

Principal (*with great interest*): What did you do?

Miss Pringle: No, no, no, it's the *topic* of the essay: what you did last summer.

Principal: Mr. Willoughby and I went to the New Jersey seashore. He was brought up there. It brings back fond memories of his childhood. Bouncing on his mother's knee. Being hugged, being kissed. Mmmmmm. Mmmmmm. (*Makes kissing sounds, hugs herself; into intercom:*) Henry, sweetie, I want you to buy my husband underwear. Pink. The bikini kind. Calvin Klein, or something like that. Or you could use your "Ah Men" catalog if it wouldn't take too long. Mr. Willoughby is a medium. Thank you, Henry. (*To* Miss Pringle:) I'm sorry, what were you saying?

Miss Pringle: About Daisy's essay.

Principal: What about it?

Miss Pringle: Well . . .

PRINCIPAL: Wait a moment, would you? (*Into intercom:*) Henry, I mean Mr. Willoughby, is a medium *size*, I don't mean he holds seances. (*Laughs; to* MISS PRINGLE:) I didn't want there to be any misunderstanding. I don't think there was, but just in case. I myself am into black magic. (*Takes out a black candle. Into intercom:*) Henry, I have taken out a black candle and I am thinking of you. (*To* MISS PRINGLE:) Do you have a match?

MISS PRINGLE: No, I'm sorry. About Daisy's essay.

PRINCIPAL: I'm all ears.

MISS PRINGLE: Well . . .

PRINCIPAL: Which is a figure of speech. As you can indeed see, I am a great deal more than just ears. I have a head, a neck, a trunk, a lower body, legs, and feet. (*Into intercom:*) I have legs and feet, Henry. I hope you're working quickly.

MISS PRINGLE: Pay attention to me! Focus your mind on what I'm saying! I do not have all day.

PRINCIPAL: Yes, I'm sorry, I will. You're right. Oh, I *admire* strong women. I've always been afraid I might actually be a lesbian, but I've never had any opportunity to experiment with that side of myself. You're not interested, are you? You're single. Perhaps you *are* a lesbian.

MISS PRINGLE: I'm not a lesbian, thank you, anyway.

PRINCIPAL: Neither am I. I just thought maybe I was. (*Into intercom:*) Henry, you don't think I'm a lesbian, do you? (*Listens.*) The intercom only works one way, it needs to be repaired. Of course, Henry's a mute anyway.

MISS PRINGLE: Mrs. Willoughby, please, put your hand over your mouth for a moment and don't say anything.

PRINCIPAL: I'm all ears. (*Puts her hand over her mouth.*)

MISS PRINGLE: Good, thank you. I was disturbed by Daisy's essay. I want you to listen to it. "What I Did For My Summer Vacation." By Daisy Dingleberry. "Dark, dank rags. Wet, fetid towels. A large German shepherd, its innards splashed across the windshield of a car. Is this a memory? Is it a dream? I am trapped, I am trapped, how to escape. I try to kill myself, but the buses always stop. Old people and children get discounts on buses, but still no one will ever kill me. How did I even learn to speak, it's amazing. I am a baked potato. I am a summer squash. I am a vegetable. I am an inanimate object who from time to time can run very quickly, but I am not really alive. Help, help, help. I am drowning, I am drowning, my lungs fill with the summer ocean, but still I do not die, this awful life goes on and on, can no one rescue me." (MISS PRINGLE *and* the PRINCIPAL *stare at one another.*) What do you think I should do?

PRINCIPAL: I'd give her an A. I think it's very good. The style is good, it rambles a bit, but it's unexpected. It's sort of an intriguing combination of Donald Barthelme and Sesame Street. All that "I am a baked potato" stuff. I liked it.

MISS PRINGLE: Yes, but don't you think the child needs help?

PRINCIPAL: Well, a good editor would give her some pointers, granted, but I think she's a long way from publishing yet. I feel she should stay in school, keep working on her essays, the school track team needs her, there's no one who runs as fast. I think this is all premature, Miss Pringle.

MISS PRINGLE: I feel she should see the school psychologist.

PRINCIPAL: I am the school psychologist.

MISS PRINGLE: What happened to Mr. Byers?

PRINCIPAL: I fired him. I thought a woman would be better suited for the job.

MISS PRINGLE: But do you have a degree in psychology?

PRINCIPAL: I imagine I do. I can have Henry check if you insist. Are you sure you're not a lesbian? I think you're too forceful, it's unfeminine. And I think you're picking on this poor child. She shows signs of promising creativity, and first you try to force her into premature publishing, and now you want to send her to some awful headshrinker who'll rob her of all her creativity in the name of some awful God of normalcy. Well, Miss Pringle, here's what I have to say to you: I will not let you rob Daisy Dingleberry of her creativity, she will not see a psychologist as long as she is in this school, and you are hereby fired from your position as teacher in this school. Good day! (*Into intercom:*) Henry, come remove Miss Pringle bodily from my office, sweetie, would you?

MISS PRINGLE: No need to do that. I can see myself out. Let me just say that I think you are insane, and I am sorry you are in a position of power.

PRINCIPAL: Yes, but I *am* in a position of power! (*Into*

intercom:) Aren't I, Henry? Now get out of here before I start to become violent.

MISS PRINGLE: I am sorry you will not let me help this child.

PRINCIPAL: Help this child! She may be the next Virginia Woolf, the next Sylvia Plath. '

MISS PRINGLE: Dead, you mean.

PRINCIPAL (*screams*): Who cares if she's dead as long as she publishes? Now, get out of here! (*Blackout.*)

S C E N E 4

A blank stage, a simple white spot. From a loud-speaker at the back of the auditorium we hear a male voice—serious, sympathetic in a detached, businesslike manner.

VOICE: Come in please.

(*Enter a young man in a simple, modest dress. His haircut, shoes, and socks, though, are traditionally masculine. He looks out to the back of the auditorium to where the voice is originating from. The young man seems shy, polite, tentative.*)

State your name please.

YOUNG MAN: Daisy.

VOICE: How old are you?

DAISY: I'm seventeen.

VOICE: I wish I had gotten your case earlier. Why are you wearing a dress?

DAISY: Oh, I'm sorry, am I? (*Looks, is embarrassed.*) I didn't realize. I know I'm a boy . . . young man. It's just I was so used to wearing dresses for so long that some mornings I wake up and I just forget. (*Thoughtfully, somewhat to himself.*) I should really just clear all the dresses out of my closet.

VOICE: Why did you used to wear dresses?

DAISY: Well, that's how my parents dressed me. They said they didn't know what sex I was, but it had to be one of two, so they made a guess, and they just guessed wrong.

VOICE: Are your genitals in any way misleading?

DAISY: No, I don't believe so. I don't think my parents ever really looked. They didn't want to intrude. It was a kind of politeness on their part. My mother is sort of delicate, and my father rests a lot.

VOICE: Did you think they acted out of politeness?

DAISY: Well, probably. It all got straightened out eventually. When I was eleven, I came across this medical book that had pictures in it, and I realized I looked more like a boy than a girl, but my mother had always wanted a girl or a best-seller, and I didn't want to disappoint her. But then some days, I don't know what gets into me, I would just feel like striking out at them. So I'd wait till she was having one of her crying fits, and I took the book to her—I was twelve now—and I said, Have you ever seen this book? Are you totally insane? Why have you named me Daisy? Everyone else has always said I was a boy, what's the *matter* with you? And she kept crying and she said something about Judith Krantz and something about being out of Shake-n-Bake chicken, and then she said, I want to die; and then she said, *perhaps* you're a boy, but we don't want to jump to any hasty conclusions, so why don't we just wait, and we'd see if I menstruated or not. And I asked her what that word meant, and she slapped me and washed my mouth out with soap. Then she apologized and hugged me, and said she was a bad mother. Then she washed *her* mouth out with soap. Then she tied me to the kitchen table and turned on all the gas jets and said it would be just a little while longer for the both of us. Then my father came home and he turned off the gas jets and untied me. Then when he asked if dinner was ready, she lay on the kitchen floor and wouldn't move, and he said, I guess not, and then he sort of crouched next to the refrigerator and tried to read a book, but I don't think he was really reading, because he never turned any of the pages. And then eventually, since nothing else seemed to be happening, I just went to bed. (*Fairly long pause.*)

VOICE: How did you feel about this?

DAISY: Well, I knew something was wrong with them. But then they meant well, and I felt that somewhere in all that, they actually cared for me—after all, she washed *her* mouth with soap too, and he untied me. And so I forgave them because they meant well. I tried to understand them. I felt sorry for them. I considered suicide.

VOICE: That's the end of the first session.

> (*Lights change. In view of the audience,* DAISY *removes his girl's clothing and changes into men's clothing—pants and a shirt, maybe a sweater. As he changes we hear the "Hush little baby" theme played rather quickly, as on a speeded-up music box. The change should be as fast and as simple as possible. Lights come up and focus on* DAISY *again.*)

This is your second session. How old are you?

DAISY: I'm nineteen now.

VOICE: Why have you waited two years between your first and second sessions? And you never called to cancel them. I've been waiting here for two years.

DAISY: I'm sorry. I should have called. I was just too depressed to get here. And I'm in college now, and I've owed this paper on Jonathan Swift and *Gulliver's Travels* for one and a half *years*. I keep trying to write it, but I just have this terrible problem *beginning* it.

VOICE: In problems of this sort, it's best to begin at the beginning, follow through to the middle, and continue on until the ending.

DAISY: Ah, well, I've tried that. But I don't seem to get very far. I'm still on the first sentence. "Jonathan Swift's *Gulliver's Travels* is a biting, bitter work that . . ." I keep getting stuck on the "that."

VOICE: I see you're wearing men's clothing today.

DAISY (*with a sense of decisiveness*): I threw all my

dresses away. And I'm going to change my name from Daisy. I'm considering Francis or Hillary or Marion.

VOICE: Any other names?

DAISY: Rocky.

VOICE: Have you seen your parents lately?

DAISY: I try not to. They call me and they cry and so on, but I hold the receiver away from my ear. And then I go next to the refrigerator and I crouch for several days.

VOICE: How are you doing in school?

DAISY: I'm not even sure I'm *registered*. It's not just the Jonathan Swift paper I owe. I owe a paper comparing a George Herbert poem with a Shakespeare sonnet; I owe a paper on characterization in *The Canterbury Tales*; and an essay on the American character as seen in Henry James's *Daisy Miller*. (DAISY *looks off into the distance, and sings softly.*)
> Daisy, Daisy,
> Give me your answer, do,
> I'm half-crazy . . .
> (*He looks grave, sad, repeats the line.*)
> I'm half-crazy . . .

(*His sadness increases, he speaks slowly.*) " 'I am half-sick of shadows,' said the Lady of Shallot."

VOICE: You sound like an English major.

DAISY (*his attention returns to the* VOICE): Yes. I learned a certain love of literature from my parents. My mother is a writer. She is the author of the Cliff Notes to *Scruples* and *Princess Daisy*. And my father liked reading. When he was next to the refrigerator, he would often read. I like reading. I have this eerie dream, though, sometimes that I'm a baby in my crib and somebody is reading aloud to me from what I think is *Mommie Dearest*, and then this great big dog keeps snarling at me, and then this enormous truck or bus or something drops down from the sky, and it kills me. (*With a half-joking, half-serious disappointment that he's not dead.*) Then I always wake up.

VOICE: That's the end of our second session.

(*The lights change abruptly. From now on, these abrupt light changes—probably a center spot with side lighting that switches side to side on each change—will represent time passing and finding* DAISY *in the midst of other sessions.*)

DAISY: Doctor, I'm so depressed I can hardly talk on the phone. It's like I can only function two hours a day at maximum. I have this enormous desire to feel absolutely nothing.

VOICE: That's the end of our third session.

(*Lights change abruptly.*)

DAISY: You know, when I *do* get up, I sleep with people obsessively. I'm always checking people out on the street to see who I can sleep with.

VOICE: Eventually you'll get a lot of venereal diseases.

DAISY: I know, I already have. It's just that during the sex, there's always ten or twenty seconds during which I forget *who I am* and *where I am*. And that's why I'm so obsessive. But it's ridiculous to spend hours and hours seeking sex just really in order to find those ten or twenty seconds. It's so *time consuming!* I mean, no wonder I never get that paper on *Gulliver's Travels* done.

VOICE: Oh, you still haven't done that paper?

DAISY: No. I've been a freshman for five years now. I'm never going to graduate. At registration every fall, people just laugh at me.

VOICE: That's the end of our fifty-third session. See you Tuesday.

(*Lights change.*)

DAISY (*incensed*): I mean it's the *inconsistency* I hate them most for! One minute they're cooing and cuddling and feeding me Nyquil, and the next minute they're turning on the gas jets, or lying on the floor, or threatening to step on my back. How *dare* they treat me like that? What's the matter with them! I didn't ask to be brought into the world. If they didn't know how to raise a child, they should have gotten a dog; or a kitten—they're more independent—or a *gerbil!* But left me *unborn*.

VOICE: That's the end of our two hundred and fifteenth session.

(*Lights change.*)

DAISY: I passed this couple on the street yesterday, and they had this four-year-old walking between them, and the two parents were fighting and you could just *tell* that they were insane. And I wanted to snatch that child from them and . . .

VOICE: And what?

DAISY: I don't know. Hurl it in front of a car, I guess. It was too late to save it. But at least it would be dead.

VOICE: That's the end of our three hundred and seventy-seventh session.

(*Lights change.*)

DAISY (*worn out by years of talking*): Look, I suppose my parents aren't actually evil, and maybe my plan of hiring a hit person to kill them is going too far. They're not evil, they're just disturbed. And they mean well. *But meaning well is not enough.*

VOICE: How's your *Gulliver's Travels* paper going?

DAISY: I'm too depressed.

VOICE: I'm afraid I'm going to be on vacation next week.

DAISY (*unwilling to discuss this*): I'm not happy with my present name.

VOICE: I'll just be gone a week.

DAISY: I wore a dress last week.

VOICE: I won't be gone that long.

DAISY: And I slept with thirty people.

VOICE: I hope you enjoyed it.

DAISY: And I can't be responsible for what I might do next week.

VOICE: Please, *please*, I need a vacation.

DAISY: All right, all right, take your stupid vacation. I just hope it rains.

VOICE: You're trying to manipulate me.

DAISY: Yes, but I mean well.

> (*Lights change. Very dark, a very pessimistic anger.*)

Doctor. I've been in therapy with you for *ten* years now. I have been a college freshman for six years, and a college sophomore for four years. The National Defense loan I have taken to pay for this idiotic education will take me a *lifetime* to repay. (*His voice sounds lost.*) I don't know. I just feel sort of, well, stuck.

VOICE: Yes?

DAISY: Oh. And I had another memory I'd forgotten, something else my parents did to me. It was during that period I stayed in the laundry pile.

VOICE (*his voice betraying a tiny touch of having had enough*): Yes?

DAISY: My mother had promised me I could have ice cream if I would just stand up for ten minutes and not lie in the laundry, and then when I did stand up for ten minutes, it turned out she had forgotten she was defrosting the refrigerator and the ice cream was all melted. (*Sighs.*) I mean, it was so typical of her. (*Suddenly starts to get heated up.*) She had a college education. *Who could forget they were defrosting the refrigerator?!?* I mean, don't you just hate her?

VOICE: How old are you?

DAISY: Twenty-seven.

VOICE: Don't you think it's about time you let go of all this?

DAISY: What?

VOICE: Don't you think you should move on with your life? Yes, your parents were impossible, but that's already happened. It's time to move on. Why don't you do your damn *Gulliver's Travels* paper? Why don't you decide on a name? My secretary has writer's cramp from changing your records from Rocky to Butch to Cain to Abel to Tootsie to Raincloud to Elizabeth the First to Elizabeth the Second to PONCHITTA PEARCE TO MARY BAKER EDDY! I mean, we know you had a rough start, but PULL YOURSELF TOGETHER! You're smart, you have resources, you can't blame them forever. MOVE ON WITH IT!

(DAISY *has listened to the above embarrassed and uncomfortable, not certain how to respond.*)

DAISY: FUCK YOU! (*Blackout.*)

S C E N E 5

The home of JOHN *and* HELEN. *A big box with a bow on it; on top of it a smaller box with a bow on it. A large banner that says,* HAPPY BIRTHDAY, PONCHITTA. JOHN *has two bottles of vodka;* HELEN *is using a Vicks inhaler.*

HELEN (*inhaling*): Mmmmmmm, I love this aroma. It almost makes me wish I had a cold. (*Inhales.*) Mmmmmmm, delicious. Oh, there are pleasurable things in life. (*Calls offstage.*) Daisy, dear, are you almost ready? We want to see how you look in your present.

JOHN: I thought his name was Ponchitta. (*Pronounced: Pon-cheat-a.*)

HELEN: John, we've been telling you all day, he called himself Ponchitta only for the month of March several years ago. He's been calling himself Charles Kuralt for the last several years, and now that he's turned thirty, as a gift to me, he's decided to go back to the name of Daisy. (*Calls.*) Daisy! We're waiting for you.

JOHN: I wish someone would've told me. I would've changed the banner.

HELEN: The banner's a lovely gesture, John. We all appreciate it. No one gives a fuck what's on it. I'm sorry, I don't mean to swear. No one gives a shit what's on it. Daisy, dear! Mommy and Daddy want to see you in your present.

> (*Enter* DAISY *wearing a Scottish kilt; he looks somewhat pained, but has decided to be polite and not make waves. He holds his pants.*)

(*Admiring the kilt.*) Ohhhhh. Do you like it, dear?

DAISY: I'm not certain.

HELEN: Now it's not a dress, I want to make that very clear. It's a Scottish *kilt*. Scottish *men* wear them in the highlands, and all that air is wonderful for your potency if you're wearing boxer shorts rather than those awful jockey shorts that destroy your semen. Isn't that so, John?

JOHN: I wasn't listening.

HELEN (*making the best of things*): That's right, you

weren't listening. None of us were. All our heads were elsewhere. (*To* DAISY:) Your father's become a Christian Scientist, and we're all so pleased. Now when he cuts himself, we don't even put a Band-Aid on him, we just watch him bleed.

JOHN (*cheerful, telling a fun anecdote*): Cut myself this morning. Shaving. A nasty slice on the bottom of my foot. Between the vodka and the Dalmane and then the weight of the razor, I fell right over. (*Laughs.*) Then trying to get up, I sliced my foot. Mother wouldn't let me put a Band-Aid on because she thinks I've become a Christian Scientist.

HELEN (*firmly*): That's right. That's what I do think. Ponchitta, dear, I'm sorry, I mean Daisy, you're so silent. Do you like your birthday present?

DAISY: Did you give this to me because you thought I'd like it because you're insane, or did you give it to me as a sort of nasty barb to remind me that you dressed me as a girl the first fifteen years of my life?

HELEN (*sincerely*): I gave it to you because I thought you'd like it. Because I'm insane. I'm insane because I stayed in a bad marriage and didn't do what I was supposed to do with my life. But I'm not bitter. And now that your father's become a Christian Scientist, I'm going to become a Jehovah's Witness and go to the supermarket *forcing* people to take copies of *The Watchtower*. Perhaps *The Watchtower* will publish me. Certainly somebody has to, someday.

JOHN: Your mother's going through a religious phase. Cocktail, anyone? (*Offers one of the bottles.*)

HELEN: Your father calls drinking from a bottle a cocktail. It's sort of adorable really. No, dear, but you have one. Oh, I'm enjoying life so much today. And you've turned thirty, and that means I'm getting nearer to death and have wasted my youth—oh, it cheers me up. Happy birthday, dear. (*Kisses* DAISY.)

JOHN: He hasn't opened up his other presents.

HELEN: Yes, Daisy dear, we have other presents. Here's one.

(DAISY *puts his pants down on the couch and opens small box. It's a can, which when opened a large "snake" pops out of, just as happened to baby in first scene.* DAISY *is startled.* HELEN *and* JOHN *laugh in delight.*)

Daisy always loved surprises. And now open the bigger box.

(DAISY *opens bigger box*—NANNY *comes springing out of the box, shrieking, much like the snake did.* DAISY *falls over backward.*)

NANNY: AAAAAAAAAAAAAGGGGGGGHHHHH!!! Whoogie! Whoogie! Whoogie! Surprise!!!!!

HELEN: Everybody sing!

HELEN, JOHN, AND NANNY (*sing, to the tune of "Frere Jacques"*):

Happy birthday, happy birthday,
Daisy dear, Daisy dear,
Happy, happy birthday,
Happy, happy birthday,
Happy birthday, happy birthday.

DAISY: *Who is this?¿¿*

NANNY: I'm your Auntie Mame! (*Laughs.*) No, just kidding. I'm the ANTICHRIST! (*Laughs.*) No, just kidding. (*Fondly.*) I'm your Auntie Nanny.

(HELEN *brings* DAISY *over to* NANNY, *who remains in the box.*)

HELEN: This is Nanny. Don't you remember Nanny?

DAISY: I remember something. God knows what. Why did you sing "Happy Birthday" to the wrong melody?

HELEN: Well, Nanny told us you have to pay a royalty to sing the real "Happy Birthday" melody. The selfish people who wrote the stupid melody don't have to lift a finger for the rest of their fucking lives, while I have to sweat and slave over the Cliff Notes to *The Thorn Birds*. (*Pause.*) And all because your father has never been able to earn a living. (*Looks at* JOHN; *says with total, grim sincerity:*) Oh why don't you just keel over and die? (*Laughs.*) Ha, ha, just kidding, I'm fine.

NANNY (*to* DAISY, *in baby-talk voice*): Hellllooooo. Hellllooooo. What pwetty bwue eyes oo have. Cooooo. Cooooo. (*Suddenly.*) SHUT UP! Comin' back to you, honey?

DAISY: Slightly. I try not to remember too much. It doesn't get me anywhere.

JOHN (*sings drunkenly, to the correct melody*): Happy birthday to you, ha—

HELEN: SHUSH! There are spies from ASCAP everywhere.

(JOHN *turns his head with some trepidation, looking for the spies.*)

NANNY: It's so nice to see one of my babies grown up. And what a pretty dress. The plaid matches your eyes.

HELEN: It's not a dress, Nanny. It's a *kilt*.

NANNY: Well, whatever it is, it's very becoming.

JOHN (*sings*): Happy birthday . . .

HELEN: Please, John, *please.* (*Starts to get tears in her voice.*) We can't afford to pay the royalty. (*Starts to cry.*)

NANNY (*to* HELEN *soothingly*): There, there. SHUT UP! Ha, ha. (HELEN *looks startled; then she and* NANNY *laugh and embrace.*) Oh, all my babies grow up so strong and healthy, I'm so pleased. What does baby do for a living?

HELEN: He goes to college. He was a freshman for six years, and he's been in sophomore slump for seven years.

NANNY: Thirteen years of college. Baby must be very smart.

HELEN: He's been having trouble writing his freshman expository writing paper on *Gulliver's Travels.* How's that going, Rocky, I'm sorry, I mean Daisy?

DAISY: I finished it. I thought I'd read it to you.

HELEN: Oh, this will be a treat. John, are you still there? John? Daisy is going to read to us.

NANNY: Let me just put on my glasses. (*Puts on her glasses, listens attentively.*)

DAISY (*reads from a sheet of paper*): "*Gulliver's Travels* is a biting, bitter work that . . . depresses me greatly."

HELEN: Oh, I like it so far.

DAISY: "By the end of the book, Gulliver has come to agree with the King of Brobdingnag's assessment that mankind is the quote 'most pernicious race of little odious vermin that nature ever suffered to crawl upon the surface of the earth,' unquote. At the end of the book, Gulliver rejects mankind and decides he prefers the company of horses to humans. We are meant to find Gulliver's disgust with humanity understandable, but also to see that he has by now gone mad. However, I find that I do not wish to write papers analyzing these things anymore, as I agree with Gulliver and find most of the world, including teachers, to be less worthwhile to speak to than horses. However, I don't like horses either, so I have decided after thirteen years of schooling that I am not meant to go to college and so I am withdrawing. Fuck your degree, I am going to become a bus driver."

HELEN: Oh I think that's excellent, I think you'll get a very good grade. John, wasn't that good? And how interesting you're going to become a bus driver. You've always been drawn to buses.

NANNY: I love buses too! I adore *all* public transportation. The danger of derailing, the closeness of the people, the smells, the dirt. I'm sort of like a bacteria!—wherever I am, I thrive. (*Smiles at* DAISY.)

DAISY: I'm glad you like the paper. I should also tell you that I'm getting married.

HELEN (*taken aback*): Married? How fascinating. John, I feel you're not participating in this conversation.

JOHN: How do you spell dipsomaniac, I wonder?

HELEN: John, you're too young to write your memoirs. Besides, I'm the writer in the family.

DAISY: I wasn't really intending to get married, but she's pregnant.

HELEN (*more taken aback*): Pregnant, how lovely.

JOHN: D-I-P . . .

HELEN: John, participate in your life now. This isn't a spelling bee, this is a parent-child discussion.

DAISY: She's the one thousand seven hundred and fifty-sixth person I've slept with, although only the eight hundred and seventy-seventh woman.

HELEN (*slight pause*): This conversation is just so interesting I don't know what to do with it.

DAISY: I don't think I love her, but then I don't use that word; and I do think I like her. And her getting pregnant just seemed sort of a sign that we should go ahead and get married. That, and the fact that I had taken her phone number.

JOHN: S-O-M . . .

NANNY (*sings*): K-E-Y, M-O-U-S-E.

JOHN: Yes, thank you.

NANNY: Well, I think it's marvelous. Congratulations, Daisy.

HELEN: Well, your father and I will have lots of advice to give you. Don't give the baby Nyquil until it's about three. We made a mistake with you.

DAISY: I don't really wish to hear your advice.

HELEN: Well, we listened to your awful paper. You can at least do us the courtesy of listening to whatever garbage we have to say.

JOHN (*looks out*): Oh, dear, here comes that owl again. (*Ducks, bats at air.*)

HELEN: Oh, your father's having problems again. John, dear, try to spell delirium tremens. That's a fun word.

JOHN: Z-B-X . . .

HELEN: No, dear, that's *way* off. Oh, God, he's going to be spelling all night long now. He's impossible to talk to when he's spelling. But, Daisy, you're here, and we'll talk, won't we? I've made you a delicious dinner. I've ordered up Chinese.

DAISY: I don't really think I can stay for dinner.

HELEN: But it's your birthday. I don't like Chinese food. What should I do with it?

DAISY: I hesitate to say.

HELEN: Pardon?

DAISY: I feel I must tell you that I've decided I don't think I should speak to you or father for a few years and see if I become less angry.

HELEN: Angry? Why are you angry?

DAISY: Let me see if I can answer that. (*Thinks.*) No, I don't think I can. Sorry. So, thank you for the kilt, and I better be going.

HELEN: Going?

NANNY: Baby, dear, let me give you some advice before you go. Get a *lot* of medical checkups. Aside from your promiscuity, your parents exposed you to lead, asbestos, and red dye number two from this little toy you had. Also, avoid acid rain, dioxin contamination, and any capsule tablets that might have cyanide in them. Try to avoid radiation and third-degree burns after the atomic explosions come. And, finally, work on having a sense of humor. Medically, humor and laughter have been shown to physically help people to cope with the tensions of modern life that can be otherwise internalized, leading to cancer, high blood pressure, and spastic colon. (*Smiles.*) Well! It was very nice to see you, best of luck in the future; and Helen, if you'd just mail me back to Eureka, California, at your earliest convenience, I'd much appreciate it. (NANNY *disappears back into her box.*)

DAISY: What toy was she talking about?

HELEN: Oh who knows? Nanny's memory is probably starting to go. She must be about a hundred and three or so by now. Resilient woman.

JOHN: D-E-L . . .

HELEN: Oh, delirium. Better start, darling.

JOHN: E-R-I . . .

DAISY: Well, I must be going now.

HELEN: Oh. Oh, stay a little longer, Daisy dear.

DAISY (*trying to be kind*): Very well. (*Sits for about a count of three.*) Well, that's about it. (*Stands again.*) I think I'll just give you this kilt back, and I'll call you in a few years if I feel less hostile.

HELEN: That would be lovely, thank you, Daisy.

> (*He gives her back the kilt. He picks up his trousers from the couch, but does not take the time to put them on, he just heads for the door. At the door he stops and looks at his mother. She looks hurt and bewildered. He looks at her with regret, and some awful combination of dislike and tenderness.*)

DAISY (*softly*): Goodbye. (DAISY *leaves.*)

HELEN (*recites, a great sense of loss in her voice*):
"How sharper than a serpent's tooth
It is to have an ungrateful child."

John, what's that from?

JOHN: D-E-L . . .

HELEN: What's that *from*, John?

JOHN: E-R-I, M-O-U-S-E. There! But what's delirimouse?

HELEN: God only knows, John. (JOHN *sees the kilt* HELEN *is holding.*)

JOHN: Oh, another kilt.

HELEN: No, dear. Daisy gave it back. He said some very rude things, and then he left.

JOHN: Oh. Maybe he was angry about the banner.

HELEN (*sarcastically*): Yes. Maybe that's it. Nonetheless, "to err is human, to forgive, divine." What's that from?

JOHN: *Bartlett's Famous Quotations.*

HELEN: Oh, you're just *useless.* Nanny, what's that from? Also, "how sharper than a serpent's tongue"— "tooth!"—what's that from?

NANNY *(from within box, irritated)*: I have nothing more to say. Send me to the post office.

HELEN: Send me to the post office. What an orderly life Nanny leads. How I envy that.

JOHN: Uh oh. *(Ducks another owl.)*

HELEN: They're low-flying little beasts, aren't they, John? John, I wonder if I'm too old to have another baby? We could try again. *(JOHN ducks again.)* But perhaps you're not in the mood tonight. Well, we can talk about it tomorrow. *(Looks sadly out, feels alone.)* "Tomorrow and tomorrow and tomorrow." *(Very sad.)* John, what's that from? Nanny? *(No response from either; she sighs.)* One loses one's classics. *(Stares out. Lights dim.)*

S C E N E 6

The bassinet from the first scene of the play in a spot. DAISY, *dressed normally in men's clothing, enters with a young woman named* SUSAN. SUSAN *is pretty and soft and sympathetic. They stand over the bassinet.*

SUSAN: Hello, baby, hello. Coooo. Coooo. It's such a cute baby. Isn't it amazing how immediately one loves them?

DAISY: Yes, I guess so.

SUSAN: Say hello to the baby, Alexander.

DAISY (*somewhat stiffly*): Hello.

SUSAN: Alexander, you're so stiff. Be more friendly to the child.

DAISY: Hello. (*He's better at it.*) Now, we do know its sex, right?

SUSAN: Yes, it's a boy. Remember we sent out that card that said "Alexander and Susan Nevsky are proud to announce the birth of their son, Alexander Nevsky, Jr."?

DAISY: Yes. *I* remember. I was just testing to check that you weren't insane and suddenly saying it was a girl.

SUSAN: No, I'm not insane. Hello, Alexander, Jr. (*To* DAISY:) How odd that you're called Alexander Nevsky. Do you have Russian ancestors?

DAISY: No. Truthfully, I took the name myself. I liked the musical score to the movie. I've always had trouble with names.

SUSAN: Well, it's a very nice name. (*Baby starts to cry.*)

DAISY: Oh, my God, it's crying.

SUSAN: Oh dear. What should we do, I wonder?

DAISY: I'm not certain. (*They pause for a while.*) Probably we should hold it.

SUSAN (*picks the baby up*): Instinctively that feels right. There, there. It's all right. It's all right. (*Baby stops crying.*)

DAISY: Goodness, how did you do that?

SUSAN: Here, you try. (*Hands him the baby.* DAISY *holds the baby rather awkwardly; the baby starts to cry.*)

DAISY: He doesn't like me.

SUSAN: Well, bounce him a little. (DAISY *does.*)

DAISY: There, there. (*Baby stops crying.*)

SUSAN: Sing to him, why don't you?

DAISY (*sings*):
    Hush, little baby, don't you cry,
    Mama's gonna give you a big black . . .

    (DAISY *thinks, stares out quietly for a moment, changes the word.*)
    . . . poodle.

SUSAN: Are those the lyrics?

DAISY: I don't know the lyrics. (*Sings.*)
    And if that big black poodle should attack,
    Mama's gonna step on your little . . .

    (*Catches himself again, redoes the whole line, making up the lyric as he goes.*)
    Mama's . . . gonna . . . teach you . . . to bite it back,
    And when baby grows up, big and strong,
    Baby . . . can help mama . . . rewrite this song.

SUSAN: That's very sweet, Alexander.

    (DAISY *looks at* SUSAN, *smiles a little. They both sing to the baby.*)

BOTH:
    Hush, little baby, don't you cry,
    Mama's gonna give you a big black poodle,

And if that big black poodle should attack,
Mama's gonna teach you to bite it back,
And when baby grows up, big and strong,
Baby can help mama rewrite this song . . .

(*They keep humming to the baby as the lights dim to black.*)

Laughing
Wild

Laughing Wild was presented by Playwrights Horizons (Andre Bishop, artistic director and Paul S. Daniels, executive director) on October 23, 1987. It was directed by Ron Lagomarsino; the set design was by Thomas Lynch; the costume design was by William Ivey Long; the lighting design was by Arden Fingerhut; the sound design was by Stan Metelits; the press representative was Bob Ullman; the production manager was Carl Mulert; and the production stage manager was M. A. Howard. The cast was as follows:

ACT I

LAUGHING WILD
    WOMAN   E. Katherine Kerr
SEEKING WILD
    MAN   Christopher Durang

ACT II

DREAMING WILD
    WOMAN   E. Katherine Kerr
    MAN   Christopher Durang

The phrase "laughing wild" occurs in Samuel Beckett's *Happy Days*, in which Winnie, who's always trying to remember her "classics" says: "Oh, well, what does it matter, that is what I always say, so long as one ... you know ... what is that wonderful line ... laughing wild ... something something laughing wild amid severest woe."

Beckett and Winnie in turn are quoting Thomas Gray and his poem "Ode on a Distant Prospect of Eton College," in which the "something something" is "and moody Madness laughing wild amid severest woe."

Act I

Laughing Wild

A Woman *enters and addresses the audience. She is dressed fairly normally. She sits in a chair and talks to the audience. She gets up from the chair from time to time when the spirit moves her. The backdrop behind her is nondescript—pretty much a limbo setting.*

Woman: Oh, it's all such a mess. Look at this mess. My hair is a mess. My clothes are a mess.

I want to talk to you about life. It's just too difficult to be alive, isn't it, and to try to function? There are all these people to deal with. I tried to buy a can of tuna fish in the supermarket, and there was this *person* standing right in front of where I wanted to reach out to get the tuna fish, and I waited a while, to see if they'd move, and they didn't—they were looking at tuna fish too, but they were taking a real long time on it, reading the ingredients on each can like they were a book, a pretty boring book, if you ask me, but nobody has; so I waited a long while, and they didn't move, and I couldn't get to the tuna fish cans; and I thought about asking them to move, but then they seemed so stupid not to have *sensed* that I needed to get by them that I had this awful fear that it would do no good, no good at all, to ask them, they'd probably say something like, "We'll move when we're goddamn ready, you nagging bitch," and then what would I do? And so then I started to cry out of frustration, quietly, so as not to disturb anyone, and still, even though I was softly sobbing, this stupid person didn't *grasp* that I needed to get by them to reach the goddamn tuna fish, people are so insensitive, I just hate them, and so I reached over with my fist, and I brought it down real hard on his head and I screamed: "Would you kindly move, asshole!!!"

And the person fell to the ground, and looked totally startled, and some child nearby started to cry, and I was still crying, and I couldn't imagine making use of the tuna fish now anyway, and so I shouted at the child to stop crying—I mean, it was drawing too much attention to me—and I ran out of the supermarket, and I thought, I'll take a taxi to the Metropolitan Museum of Art, I need to be surrounded with culture right now, not tuna fish.

But you know how hard it is to hail a taxi. I waved my hand, and then this terrible man who came to the street *after* I was there waved his hand, and the taxi stopped for him because he saw him first, and the injustice of it made my eyes start to well with tears again. So I lost that taxi. So I raised my hand again, and the next *three* taxis were already full, although one of them still had his "free" light on, which made me angry, because if he had had it off, I probably wouldn't have raised my arm, which was getting tired now, I think hitting the man with the tuna fish used some muscles I wasn't used to using. And then this other taxi started to get near, and this woman with groceries came out, and she started to hail it and I went right over to her and I shouted smack into her ear: "If you take this taxi from me, I will kill you!" And she looked really startled, and then the taxi stopped, and I got in, and I said, I want to go crosstown to the Metropolitan Museum of Art, I must have culture, and quiet, and things of value around me, I have had a terrible time in the supermarket. And then the taxi driver, who was Greek or Muslim or Armenian or something, said to me, I have to go *down*town now, I'm about to get off work.

Well, I thought my head would explode. I mean, was his taxi available, or wasn't it? And wasn't it *law* that they can't refuse you, even if you want to go to Staten Island? But I just couldn't bear the thought of pressing charges against this man—it would take days and days of phone calls, and meetings, and letters, and all because he wouldn't bring me to the goddamn Metropolitan. So I sat in his taxi and I wouldn't move. I thought for a while about going back and following through on my initial impulse to buy a can of tuna fish—tuna fish, mixed with mayonnaise, is one of the few things I can make in the kitchen—but then I realized that probably whoever was at the cash register would give me difficulties, probably because I was a woman, or because she was a woman, or maybe it was a man who hated women, or wished he was a woman—anyway it all started to seem far too complicated; so I thought, I'll just stay in this taxi cab, and I'll be damned if I get out. And he kept saying, "Lady, please, I have to get home to my family." And I said, "Where? In Staten Island?"

And then I thought, I won't even argue, I'll just sit here. And he started to shout at me, obscenities and so on, and I thought, well, at least I'm sitting down, maybe eventually he'll decide it's easier just to drive me to the Metropolitan; although I started to think maybe I didn't want to go there anyway, I was hungry, for starters, maybe a movie with popcorn and Diet Coke and those chocolate-covered ice-cream balls, what are they called—they're delicious, and they cost about two-fifty in the movie theater, which is ridiculously expensive—but then what movie would I see; and then all of a sudden he pulled his cab out into traffic in a great big hurry, it made me sort of lurch in my seat, and I yelled out, "I've changed my mind, I want to see a movie"; and before I could ask him for recommendations, he said he was taking me to the police station, and I thought, yes, but isn't he in the wrong, refusing a fare? But then you know the stories you've read about police brutality and all, maybe they'd have one of those electrical devices, and they'd shock me even though I wasn't Puerto Rican—well, whatever, I didn't think going to the police was worth it as a risk, so when he stopped at a stop light—violently, I might add, there's probably something wrong with my back, I could sue, but litigation is so complicated and here I can't even buy a can of tuna— I swung the cab door open and I shouted into his open window, "Your mother sucks cocks in hell!" Although I think my tongue slipped and I actually said, "Your mother sucks socks in hell," which was kind of funny, but I was too angry to laugh; and he just said, "You're fuckin' nuts," and he drove off in this terrible hurry, and the tire almost went over my foot, but luckily I fell backwards into the gutter. (*Looks at the audience for a moment.*)

Are you all following this so far?

Have you ever noticed how spring is lovely, but it fills one with sad longing because nothing in one's life will ever live up to the sweet feelings it raises, and that fall is lovely but that it fills one with sad longing because everything is dying; and life is beautiful and awful and there's no assuagement of this awful longing inside one? Have you all noticed this? I presume it's a universal feeling, isn't it? I know I feel it's universal.

(*With renewed energy.*) So, there I was lying on my back in the gutter, and this street musician came over to me and he asked me if I needed help, and I said, "No, but can you play 'Melancholy Baby'?" And I thought that that was a pretty funny thing for me to say under the circumstances, and that I had a fair wit and intelligence even if I had been in mental institutions, and I thought to myself, maybe if this man laughs at my comment, which is wry and peculiar and yet oddly appropriate to the circumstance, that maybe I will have found a companion for the rest of my life, to help me find spring and fall less painful, summer's too hot, I wouldn't expect anyone to be able to help with that, and winter has gotten less cold than it was when I was a child, it's probably something terrible the captains of industry have done to the atmosphere, probably some ozone layer has been thinned out beyond repair, and the sun is coming through more directly, and we'll all die from it and get skin cancers, and breathe wrong things through our nostrils ... oh God, I mustn't worry about things that may not be true and that I can't do anything about anyway. Besides which, this street musician didn't laugh at my comment about "Melancholy Baby," he looked at me very seriously and asked me if I was all right, and I said, "You don't really want to know, do you? You don't want to know how I am really, to hold me in the night, to comfort me in sickness and in health," sickness caused by the dying of the ozone layer, health caused by ... well, who knows what causes health, probably sugar is killing all of us, and besides, I hadn't really even gotten a good look at him in the dark, maybe I wouldn't like his looks, he might not be the right person for me to spend the rest of my life with anyway. And then he asked me if I wanted help to stand up or if I wanted to stay seated in the gutter, and I thought to myself, I don't know the answer to this question. And so I said, with a laugh, "I don't know the answer to that question, ask me another one," which I thought was kind of a funny remark in the circumstances, this crazy lady in the gutter after she's attacked someone at the tuna fish counter and been assaulted by a taxi driver, sort of gallant and witty in the midst of unspeakable woe.

What is that line from Beckett? "Laughing wild amid severest woe."

So then I said to him, with another wry smile, "I am laughing wild amid severest woe." And he looked at me blankly, and I said, "I am laughing wild!" And since he didn't seem to get it, I threw back my head, and I let out this enormous, frightening laugh I do at parties: AHAHAHAHAHAHAHAHAHAHAH! And he looked alarmed and then he said, if you need help getting to the ladies' shelter, I'll be over there playing my guitar. And then I knew I'd been fortune's fool, that this man was not meant to share my life with me, he was humorless, he didn't have a sense of shared existential ennui, angst, whatever, I've been to college. Although I didn't read everything they assigned me, of course. What good would it have done? (*Looks at the audience.*)

Do you follow me so far? Do you feel a kinship, or are you looking at me like that street musician did?

You know, sometimes I love street musicians—not that particular one, of course, but sometimes if one is walking down the grubby street, like yesterday I was, and this young girl was playing a cello, all by herself, it was late, it was dark, the city was filled with horrible people—outpatients from Creedmoor, some of whom I know; horrible teenagers from New Jersey who come on dates pretending that life is *wonderful*—they'll learn, I hope they cry a hundred tears—I have this hostility toward anyone who is happy. But I do appreciate beauty, and the strains of melancholy comfort rising from this young woman's cello brought a momentary peace to my soul. I stood for a moment and listened in awe, and then I gave her a nickel. You may think that was cheap, but it was a nickel bag of coke. AHAHAHAHAHA-HAHA!

No, I'm kidding, it was just a nickel, five cents. I only listened to it for a moment, I can't be expected to support the woman, she plays well, why doesn't she get a job in the state symphony and not be out and about on the streets, irritating everyone, making them feel guilty? No, but that contradicts the point I was making. I love street musicians. (*She sings something light and pretty, for example a bit of "Vilia" from Franz Lehar's* The Merry Widow.)

You may ask, what parties has she gone to to unleash this peculiar laugh? Mostly the Warhol crowd. One of the orderlies at Creedmoor said to me, "You remind me of Edie Sedgwick, I bet Andy Warhol would like you." This was before he died, of course. And so one of the times I wasn't institutionalized I went to a party that Warhol was at, supposedly, but I never met him. That's why I haven't had the film career Edie Sedgwick had. But I haven't minded really. I think film takes away a little bit of your soul each time you're photographed. That was the theme of Ibsen's *When We Dead Awaken*, only it was about sculptors, not filmmakers. I wonder if Ibsen would have liked me. I wonder if I would have liked Ibsen. I'm glad I never met Strindberg, I probably would've married him. I have a bad instinct about these sorts of things. Although who should I marry? Alan Alda? I liked him for about five minutes, but now I think he's a pill. Have you ever noticed that after you've known someone for just a little while how intolerable you find them?

And speaking of which, who is Sally Jessy Raphael? Does anyone know? I have a television in my apartment, I don't have a bed, but I have trouble sleeping anyway, sometimes I sleep in the bathtub, and she's on at three in the morning, that is, Sally Jessy Raphael is, and in some of the promos I've seen her pose with Phil Donahue, and she runs a talk show sort of like his, so I suppose she's supposed to be a kind of female Phil Donahue. But my point is, who is she? Why does she think she's interesting, or that we should listen to her? Why does she have all this self-confidence? Why doesn't she have the humility to know she's not so special? I don't have self-confidence. I think I'm special, but I have sufficient humility to question myself, maybe I'm totally worthless. But even at my most confident, I'd never try to pass myself off as a female Phil Donahue.

Plus, of course, when you're Phil Donahue you have to have opinions on so many things. I could never be president because of this. Plus, of course, if McGovern's running mate had to drop out because of shock treatments, they'd really be able to go to town with my mental history. My mental history is something, alright. I make the Frances Farmer story look like *Laugh In*. I make *The Snake Pit* look like *The Love Bug*. I make *I Never Promised You a Rose Garden* look like "Tie a Yellow Ribbon Round the Old Oak Tree." I make the dawn come up like thunder. Why did I say that? (*Thinks.*)

I wonder if it's because "Tie a Yellow Ribbon Round the Old Oak Tree" was sung by Tony Orlando and Dawn, ergo "dawn like thunder," in which case my unconscious mind is really active, isn't it? . . . Useless, but active.

I had such high hopes once. AHAHAHAHAHAHAHA-HAHA! She said, throwing her head back, madly. Laughing wild amid severest woe.

But what I said about having opinions—people with opinions usually pretend they know what should be done about things. I think that's hubris. Do you all know what hubris is? That's conceit, when you think you're as good as the gods. Well, everybody in this country has hubris. I'd like to take all the unwanted children in the world who some right-to-lifer keeps from being aborted and send them all to Mother Theresa. Let her cope with the screaming, squalling little infants; she said in some interview that people who didn't want their children should send them to her rather than have an abortion. I'd like to see her dealing with three thousand shrieking infants yelling nonstop for days on end, then I hope she'd be sorry for saying such a goody-goody, disgusting thing.

I wish I had been killed when I was a fetus. It wasn't legal then, and my mother didn't think of it, but I think she'd prefer I'd never been born. I know I'd prefer she'd never have been born, and that would have taken care of my not being born as well. Plus, I'm really sick of Mother Theresa, aren't you? I mean, what makes her such a saint? She's just like Sally Jessy Raphael, only different. Oh, God, I'm starting to ramble. But I can't

help it. And what does the A.A. prayer say? God help me
to accept the things I cannot change. I can't change my
rambling. Plus I'm not an alcoholic anyway; I just went
there because I didn't know what else to do with my
life, and I thought if I told them all I was an alcoholic
they'd accept me. But it didn't help. They say if you
don't believe in God, you just have to believe in a higher
power than yourself, but that didn't help me particularly. I mean, who? Phil Donahue? Mother Theresa?
The god Dionysus? And there was this woman at A.A.
who came and said she had stopped drinking but her life
hadn't been working out anyway, and how her parents
were alcoholics too, and she seemed very intense and
kind of crazy, and it was hard to look at her because she
was missing a tooth right in front, it didn't make for an
attractive package at all; and she talked about how the
program had helped her realize she was powerless over
alcohol, and this seemed to make her happy for some
reason or other, although I think I'm powerless over lots
of things and it doesn't make me happy; and then I
shouted out real loud at the top of my lungs: WHY
DON'T YOU GET YOUR TOOTH FIXED? And everyone looked at me real angry, and I looked embarrassed,
and then I shouted: JUST A SUGGESTION. And everyone looked uncomfortable, and there was silence for
about half an hour, and then the meeting was over,
though we all said the A.A. prayer again; and then nobody would speak to me. But lots of people went to
speak to the woman without the tooth, sort of like to
prove that they didn't care she was missing her tooth;
but then this one person came over to me, and said not
to drink the punch, and he said that he agreed with me
and that the woman looked awful; and that further-
more he'd been going to meetings for a long time, and
that this woman had been missing her tooth for several

years, and clearly had not organized herself into fixing this, and so he agreed with me wholeheartedly. And then he and I went to a hotel room and fucked, and then I tried to jump out the window, and then I went to Creedmoor for the third time. (*Looks thoughtful.*)

Have you all wondered why sexual intercourse sometimes makes you want to commit suicide? That is a universal feeling, isn't it? Or is it just me? Can I see a show of hands?

Oh, well, don't worry, I'm not one of those people who force audience participation. I'm not going to stand up here and insist you sing "Those Were the Days" and then when I've bullied you into it, complain you didn't sing loud enough, and then make you sing again. I've seen Pearl Bailey and Diana Ross do that, it's really obnoxious. I want to see them killed.

Tell me, are you enjoying my company, or are you wishing I'd go away? I can never tell in life, it's one of my problems. Reality testing of any sort is a mystery to me, my doctors say. I have the most wonderful doctors, they're all like Dr. Ruth Westheimer on television. Have you seen how she's listed in the *TV Guide*? It says, *Good Sex*, dash, Dr. Ruth Westheimer. And they wonder why I have reality testing problems. What could that mean on television, I wonder. Andy Warhol said everyone would be famous for fifteen minutes in the twentieth century, but she's already been famous for far longer than that, it doesn't look like she's ever going to go away. Eventually we'll see her on *Password* where no matter what word she's trying to communicate, she'll only talk sex. Say, the word is "nicotine." Her first clue will be "clitoris." Then "stimulation." Then "cunnilingus." Her partner will be totally baffled, especially when the host says,

"No, Marjorie, I'm sorry, the word was 'nicotine.'"
Then Dr. Ruth will laugh like crazy, just like me.
AHAHAHAHAHAHAHAHA!

(*Suddenly angry, and for real.*) But her partner will have
lost the game thanks to her stupid clues. She won't
receive the seven hundred dollars for the first round, she
will not win the trip for two to the Caribbean, to stay at
the luxurious Hyatt Regency, she will not get to move
on to the speed round where she could win thirty thousand dollars if she can guess eight words in thirty seconds, all because this nutty, smutty doctor thinks she's
cute, and thinks she knows something about something, and has hubris like every other fucking creature
in this stupid, horrible universe. *I want Dr. Ruth Westheimer and Mother Theresa to fight to the death in the
coliseum!!!*—using knives and swords and heavy metal
balls with spikes on them! And then when one of them
has her sword to the other one's throat, I want to raise
my hand and give the "thumbs down" sign just like
Siskel and Ebert dismissing a particularly dreadful
movie; and then I want Ronald Reagan hung upside
down over sulphur emissions and made to inhale toxic
waste, just like those animals who are made to smoke
three million cigarettes; and then I want Mayor Koch
made to *eat* Westway; and then I want the world to
come to a complete and total end, ka-plooey, ka-ploppy,
ka-plopp! AHAHAHAHAHAHAHAHAHAHAHA-
HAHA!

Do you get how I feel? Do you identify in some way, or
are you rejecting me? Would any of you give me a job
ever? I can't believe you would.

Because I have tried to improve my life, I have fought, I
have called people on the phone and screamed at them,

"LET ME BABY-SIT WITH YOUR CHILDREN, I PROMISE I WON'T KILL THEM," but then they don't hire me. I've called editors at Doubleday and Knopf and St. Martin's Press even, and I've said to them over the telephone, "I DON'T KNOW HOW TO TYPE AND I'M TOO UNSTABLE TO READ, BUT IF YOU HIRE ME TO BE AN ASSISTANT EDITOR I COULD TRY TO BE MORE STABLE, HUH, WHADDYA SAY?"

But do they hire me ever? What do you think? No? If you think no, raise your hand. I want to see how many of you think no. I WANT SOME AUDIENCE PARTICIPATION HERE, RAISE YOUR GODDAMN HANDS! That's better. And that's right, the answer is no. Now I want everyone to hold hands and sing "Give Peace a Chance." No, I'm kidding, I said I hated audience participation and so I do.

The word is flashlight. Dr. Ruth's clues are: "clitoris," "erect nipple," "mound of Venus," "pound of penis." AHAHAHAHAHA, I didn't know I was going to say that.

But, Dr. Ruth, I can't get the word "flashlight" from those clues. You're not helping me to win the prize. I can't get the prize with those clues. (*Starts to cry.*) I can't get the prize with those cloooooooooeeess. Oh God, I want to die, I want to die. (*Cries violently. Silence for a bit; her crying subsides.*) Uh, it's quite a relief having me silent for a while, isn't it? (*Smiles or laughs a bit, and continues to be silent.*)

My favorite book is *Bleak House*. Not the book, but the title. I haven't read the book. I've read the title. The title sounds the way I feel. And my most recent accomplishment was getting up out of the gutter after I fell down leaving that crazy taxi driver. And my Scotch is Dewar's White Label.

I feel terribly sorry for my doctors. My doctors get exhausted listening to me, I can tell they feel my words are charging out of my mouth and trying to invade their brain cells, and they're frightened. Understandably. And that's why I try to practice being quiet from time to time. Let me be quiet for a second again. (*She is quiet.*)

You see, you need that rest too, don't you?

Here is the key to existence. Are you all listening? Here is the key to existence; when I tell you this you will know how to run your lives. You will know if you have been living life to the full, and if you realize you haven't been, you will know immediately how to correct that state of affairs. As soon as I tell you the key to existence. Are you ready? Are you ready for me to tell you?

Oh, dear, I've built it up too much, and it's really not all that significant. But it's what I got from the est training: *Always breathe.* That's the basis of life, breathing. That's basically the basis. If you don't breathe, you die. (*Pause.*)

Well, it seemed more impressive when you hadn't slept for two days. If you're rested, it doesn't sound so important, but I try to hold on to it.

The other major thing I have learned is ... (*sincerely*) well, I've forgotten it, so it couldn't have been too significant.

Let me try to summarize what I've told you, and then I'll remove myself from your presence. I had trouble buying tuna fish, then I had an argument with a taxi driver, I fell in the gutter, I like street musicians sometimes, I have a startling laugh, Ahahahahaha, I don't like Sally Jessy Raphael, Mother Theresa, or Dr. Ruth Westheimer, I am opposed to "hubris," I wish I had never been born, I have trouble getting a job, I haven't read *Bleak House* but I like the title, and I have learned that you should always breathe.

Oh, and I feel great hostility toward teenagers from New Jersey who seem happy. I mentioned that earlier, didn't I? I think I did.

Well, then, I've covered everything I intended to. Thank you for giving me your attention. Goodbye, I love you. Of course, that's a lie. Some of you I think are first-class fools, and I hate you. In fact, I probably don't like any of you. Curse you! I curse all of you! May your children have webbed feet, and all your house pets get mange and worms! AHAHAHAHAHA!

I'm terribly sorry. I really can't leave you that way. The management would be so cranky if I cursed the audience right at the end of my speech, so forget I said that. I do love you. M-wah! I want to be a responsible member of this society, so give me a job if you can, I'm sure I can do *some*thing. I love you, m-wah! The ushers will give you my phone number, and the box office will field any job offers you call in. Thank you. Goodbye. Goodbye. I hope your lives are better than mine. Laugh laugh laugh laugh—I'm getting too tired to do the real laugh right now. Laugh laugh laugh. Laughing is a tonic. So forget crying. Cry, and you cry alone. Laugh and you . . . cry alone later.

And remember—always breathe. Even if I stop, you keep breathing out there, alright? Keep breathing. In and out. In and out. In and out. (*She breathes in and out several times in a somewhat exaggerated manner, as if*

to show the audience how. She then stops the exaggerated breathing, and looks at the audience for a few
beats. She's either holding her breath or, more likely,
just breathing regularly, as the lights dim.)

Seeking Wild

A space in which a talk is about to be given, i.e., a
lecture hall, a stage, or a room. There is a dark
curtain mid-stage. In front of the curtain stage
right is a chair next to a table. On the table is a
water pitcher and a glass. Stage left is a col-
umnlike stand (a pedestal), on which there are
three crystals: a large, jagged, clear crystal; a
chunk of amethyst (which is purple); a piece of
citrine (amber-colored).

Hanging on the curtain (upstage center) and
dominating the stage is a very large hand-
painted canvas poster of an Egyptian Eye. The
poster may be patterned after the Eye of Ra (or
"Horus card") found in the book The Way of Car-
touche. It is a large eye, with a primitive, bold
look to it. Beneath the eye there is a small line
(where "circles under your eyes" would be on a
person) underneath which "hangs" a stylized,
primitive design, possibly forming little icicles or
teardrops.

After a few beats, a MAN enters. The MAN is
dressed well, maybe even a little trendy. He is
dressed up to give a talk, to share his new

thoughts. He carries with him a few file cards that he has made notes on. He smiles at the audience briefly, checks his first note card quickly before beginning, and then speaks with earnestness and purpose.

MAN: I used to be a very negative person. But then I took this personality workshop that totally turned my life around. Now when something bad or negative happens, I can see the positive. Now when I have a really bad day, or when someone I thought was a really good friend betrays me, or maybe when I've been hit by one of those damn people riding bicycles the opposite way on a one-way street, so, of course, one hadn't looked in that direction and there they are bearing down on you, about to kill or maim you—anyway, I look at any of these things and I say to myself: this glass is not half full, it's half empty.

No—I said it backwards, force of habit. This glass is not half empty, it is half *full*.

Of course, if they hit you with the stupid bicycle your glass will not be half full or half empty, it will be shattered to pieces, and you'll be dead or in the hospital.

But really I'm trying to be positive, that's what I'm doing with my life these days. (*Reads from a note card.*) I was tired of not being joyful and happy, I was sick of my personality, and I had to change it.

(*Off the card; back to speaking extemporaneously.*) Half full, *not* half empty. I had to say to myself: you do not have cancer—at least not today. You are not blind. You are not one of the starving children in India or China or in Africa. Look at the sunset, look at the sunrise, why don't you enjoy them, for God's sake? And now I do. (*Almost as a sidetrack to himself.*) Except if it's cloudy, of course, and you can't see the sun. Or if it's cold. Or if it's too hot.

(*Hearing his negativity above.*) I probably need to take a few more personality workshops to complete the process. It's still not quite within my grasp, this being positive business.

(*Reads from cards again.*) But I'm making great strides. My friends don't recognize me. (*Smiles.*)

(*Off the cards again.*) And it is hard for me to be positive because I'm very sensitive to the vibrations of people around me, or maybe I'm just paranoid. But in any case, I used to find it difficult to go out of the house sometimes because of coming into contact with other people.

You've probably experienced something similar—you know, the tough on the subway who keeps staring at you and you're the only two people in the car and he keeps staring and after a while you think, does he want to kill me? Or just intimidate me? Which is annoying enough.

Or the people in movie theaters who talk endlessly during the opening credits so you can just *tell* they're going to talk through the entire movie and that it will be utterly useless to ask them not to talk.

And even if you do ask them not to talk and they ungraciously acquiesce, they're going to send out vibrations that they hate you all during the entire film, and then it will be impossible to concentrate.

You can move, but the person next to you in the new location will probably, you know, rattle candy wrappers endlessly all through the movie. Basically I don't go to the movies anymore. What's the point?

But even if you can skip going to the movies, you pretty much have to go to the supermarket.

(*Steps closer to the audience.*) I was in the supermarket the other day about to buy some tuna fish when I sensed this very disturbed presence right behind me. There was something about her focus that made it very clear to me that she was a disturbed person. So I thought— well, you should never look at a crazy person directly, so I thought, I'll just keep looking at these tuna fish cans, pretending to be engrossed in whether they're in oil or in water, and the person will then go away. But instead *wham!* she brings her fist down on my head and screams: "Would you move, asshole!" (*Pause.*)

Now why did she do that? She hadn't even said, "Would you please move" at some initial point, so I would've known what her problem was. Admittedly I don't always tell people what I want either—like the people in the movie theaters who keep talking, you know, I just give up and resent them—but on the other hand, I don't take my fist and go wham! on their heads!

I mean, analyzing it, looking at it in a positive light, this woman probably had some really horrible life story that, you know, kind of explained how she got to this point in time, hitting me in the supermarket. And perhaps if her life—*since birth*—had been explained to me, I could probably have made some sense out of her action and how she got there. But even with that knowledge— which I didn't have—it was *my* head she was hitting, and it's just so unfair.

It makes me want to never leave my apartment *ever ever again.* (*Suddenly he closes his eyes and moves his arms in a circular motion around himself, round and round, soothingly.*)

I am the predominant source of energy in my life. I let go of the pain from the past. I let go of the pain from the present. In the places in my body where pain lived previously, now there is light and love and joy. (*He opens his eyes again and looks at the audience peacefully and happily.*)

That was an affirmation.

Now the theory of affirmations is that by saying something positive about yourself in the present tense—as if the positive thing is already happening—you draw in positive energies to you. For instance, who do you think will have the easier life? Someone who goes around saying inside their head, "Everyone hates me, they try to avoid me, my job stinks, my life is miserable." Or the person who says, "Everyone likes me exactly as I am, every time I turn around people offer me friendship and money, my life is delightful and effortless." (*Pause.*)

Obviously, the second person will be much happier.

There's an additional theory that by thinking negatively, you actually cause, and are thus responsible for, the bad things that happen to you. Thus I need to look at whether I maybe *caused* the woman in the tuna fish aisle to hit me on the head. Or, since that sounds rather blaming, I need to look at the incident and see how else I could have behaved so she might *not* have hit me on the head.

When I sensed her presence, rather than doing nothing and pretending I didn't *notice* that she seemed odd, maybe I could have said, "Is something the matter?" Then maybe she would have said, "Yes, you're in my way," and I would have moved. Or, if when I said, "Is something the matter?" she stayed hostile and said,

"Why???" defensively or something, if I stayed honest and said . . . "Well, you seem odd," or, "I sense you're distressed," she might have felt that I was "responding" to her as another human being, and that might have relaxed her, and *then* she might have told me what was the matter.

So you see, I shouldn't feel like a victim. We have power.

(*Reads from his note cards.*) We can change our own thoughts, from negative to positive. (*Off the cards again, explaining.*) Say I feel bad; I can *choose* to feel good.

How do I feel right now? (*Thinks.*) I feel fine. Everything's fine. Of course, that's just on the surface, underneath there's always this gnawing residue of anxiety. But is feeling anxious just part of the human condition? Or do I feel more anxious than one should normally due to some psychological maladjustment or something? Maybe I wasn't breast-fed enough as an infant. Actually I don't even know if I was breast-fed at all. (*Thinks with concern about his lack of knowledge concerning this.*) Oh well, enough about breast feeding.

(*A surge of positive energy.*) Let me try to *change* how I feel. Let me try to feel happy for a moment. (*Closes his eyes, puts his fingers to his forehead and "flicks away" negative energy; waits for happiness.*)

No, I was just thinking about Chernobyl. That's like a scream from the universe warning us, but we're not paying attention. I can't believe they don't know what to do with nuclear waste, and then they keep building these things. I'm sorry, I was trying to feel happy. Let me try again. (*Closes his eyes, tries again.*)

Sorry, I was just thinking of something else, something I read in the newspaper about this fourteen-year-old boy in Montana who shot his geometry teacher—*to death*—because the teacher was flunking him. Now that's crazy enough, but it seems that this particular teacher didn't come to school that day, and so this four-teen-year-old boy shot the substitute teacher instead. Shot her dead. I don't know how to cope with that.

I mean, positive thinking aside, how do you protect yourself from these sorts of things? (*Suddenly wants some water, goes up to table and pours himself some while he's on this tangent of upset and negativity.*)

And there's acid rain and something wrong with the ozone layer, and the secretary of education doesn't want schools to educate students about the dangers of nu-clear proliferation, but instead to focus on how terrible the communists are. And the secretary of the environ-ment isn't in favor of protecting the environment, doesn't see a problem. The appointments to these of-fices in the Reagan administration seem like a sick joke ... like naming Typhoid Mary the secretary of health and welfare. God, it's discouraging. (*Drinks water.*)

And think about God. You know, it was nice to believe in God, and an afterlife, and I'm sometimes envious of the people who seem comfortable because they still have this belief. But I remember when everybody won Tonys for *Dreamgirls*, and they all got up there thank-ing God for letting them win this award, and I was thinking to myself: God is silent on the Holocaust, but he involves himself in the Tony awards? It doesn't seem very likely. (*Feels a need for affirmation; does the circu-lar arm motions again.*)

I am the predominant source of my life. I release anger from my solar plexus. It is replaced by serenity and white light and joy and . . . serenity. Everything in my life works. Except the plumbing and career and relationships. (*Laughs at his joke, then talks sincerely.*)

I'm sorry, I was planning on being positive out here, and it's just not happening. But I guess whatever happens is okay. Is that right?

This personality workshop I took taught me that I judge things too much, that some things just "are," you don't have to label them. And also that you shouldn't judge feelings.

This workshop also said to forgive yourself for what you haven't achieved. For instance, I had wanted to be a university professor, maybe in New England somewhere—summers off, tutorials, sherry. I'm very verbal, and that would have been a good thing to do with it.

Instead I work for a magazine, not a bad job, but not great—it's sort of a cross between . . . *TV Guide* and pornography. Well, that's too strong—but I do have to interview people who are on television series, and if they're at all attractive, they have them photographed with their blouses undone or with their shirts off. Sometimes I have nightmares about the upper bodies of Barbara Bach and Lorenzo Lamas. People whose first and last names begin with the same letter. Lorenzo Lamas. Erik Estrada. Suzanne Somers. Cher. (*Time for another affirmation.*)

Everything unfolds in my life exactly as it should, including my career. Abundance is my natural state of being, and I accept it now. I let go of anger and resentment. (*A sudden addition to the affirmation.*) I love the woman in the tuna fish aisle. I accept her exactly as she is. I accept myself exactly as I am. I approve of my body.

(*Makes equivocal face.*) I approve of *other* people's bodies.

You know, I don't like meeting people who are too attractive, and not just TV stars at my job, but anyone who's good-looking or charismatic. I hate being attracted to people, it's exhausting. It stirs up longing.

Of course, one can just do one's best to have sex with the person, and that assuages some of the longing. But the problem is, that sexual longing has no real assuagement ever, it's like longing for the moon; you can never have the moon no matter what you do, and if you were foolish enough to take a spaceship up there—and if the people running NASA didn't see to it that you were killed—you would just find that the moon was this big chunk of nothing that had nothing to do with what you were longing for at all. Oh, Olga, let's go to Moscow, and all that. There is no Moscow, there is no moon, there is no assuagement of longing.

(*Affirmation.*) I let go of my need for longing. I let go of sexual interest. I become like Buddha, and want nothing. (*Abruptly stops, to audience:*) Do these affirmations sound right to you? They sound off to me. And I've certainly never successfully acted them out. 'Cause as soon as sexual attraction kicks in, the zen in one's nature flies out the window. You meet someone, sometimes they really are terrific, other times they're just awful but nonetheless you find yourself attracted to them anyway, knowing you're an utter fool and will be very sorry later on. And then the pursuit begins. All those opening weeks of interested conversation, with the eyes more lively than usual, and each party finding the other's comments and insights more than usually charming and delightful. And then if you've been in therapy like me, there are the flirtatious exchanges of childhood traumas—all of my family were borderline schizophrenic, they beat me, they had terrible taste in furniture—and after a while one's mind starts to reverberate with, when will I have an orgasm with this person?

If there is a God, his design about sex is certainly humiliating. It's humiliating to want things. And sex itself people say is beautiful—but is it? Maybe you think it is. Terrible viscous discharges erupting in various openings may strike you as the equivalent of the Sistine Chapel ceiling, for all I know. It doesn't strike me that way. (*He stops. He realizes how extreme and cranklike his comments have begun to sound. He smiles at the audience, wanting to reestablish his rapport and his reasonability with them.*)

But I am being negative again. And clearly sex isn't just disgusting. I know that, and you know that. And when I'm lucky enough to go off with someone to his or her apartment, I certainly anticipate a pleasant time. (*Now he stops dead. He had no intention of going into this area of his life with this audience, and he's suddenly uncertain how he even got into it. Or, more to the point, how he can get out of it. He thinks, can't come up with any way to camouflage or take back what he's just said. For better or for worse, he decides just to speak honestly.*)

As the "his or her" comment suggests, I am attracted to women and to men. Though more frequently to other guys, which I find rather embarrassing to admit to publicly. Why do I bring it *up* publicly then, you may well ask? Well . . . I don't know. Why not? All my relatives are dead, and those that aren't I'm willing not to talk to.

And things like the recent Supreme Court ruling that sex between consenting adult homosexuals *not* be included in what's considered the rights of privacy—this makes me think it's now important to be open about this. Look, I've even brought pictures of myself in bed with people! (*Pats his inside jacket pocket.*) At intermission the ushers will let you look at them! ... Although I suppose the Meese Commission will run in here and try to take them away from you and then force you to buy milk at a Seven-Eleven store. God, I took some Valium before I came out here, but it hasn't calmed me down a bit.

Anyway, I didn't mean to get into this ... (*puts his note cards away in his jacket*) but I find the Supreme Court's ruling on this issue deeply disturbing. I mean, so much of the evil that men do to one another has at its core the inability of people to *empathize* with another person's position. Say when you're seven, you find yourself slightly more drawn to Johnny than you are to Jane. This is not a conscious decision on your part, it just happens, it's an instinct like ... liking the color blue.

Now in less tolerant times, you were put to death for this attraction. As time went on, this punishment was sometimes reduced to mere castration, or just imprisonment. Until recently this attraction was considered so horrific that society pretty much expected you to lie to yourself about your sexual and emotional feelings, and if you couldn't do that, certainly expected you to *shut up* about it and go live your life bottled up and terrified; and if you would be so kind as to never have any physical closeness with anyone *ever*, when you were buried you could know that society would feel you had handled your disgraceful situation with tact and willpower. That was one *cheery* option—nothing, and then the grave.

Or, you might make a false marriage with some woman who wouldn't know what was going on with you, and you could *both* be miserable and unfulfilled. That was *another* respectable option. Or you might kill yourself. There's not a lot of empathy evident in the people who prefer these options. (*He takes out his note cards again, starts to look at them, but then his mind isn't ready to leave this topic yet.*)

I mean, *I* certainly realize how insane it would be to ask a heterosexual to deny his or her natural sexual feelings and perform homosexual acts that went against *their* nature. If I can have that empathy, why can't others have the same empathy in reverse? I want some empathy here! (*Goes into an affirmation.*) I am the predominant source of . . . well, fuck that. (*Throws his note cards over his shoulder, drives on ahead.*)

And then, of course, there are all the religious teachings about homosexuality. The Book of Leviticus, for instance, says that homosexuals should basically be put to death. It also tells you how to sacrifice rams and bullocks and instructs you not to sit in a chair sat in by any woman who's had her period in the last seven days or something. To me, this is not a book to look to for much modern wisdom. (*If the audience laughs, he might smile with them.*)

People's concepts of God are so odd. For instance, take the Christians—"take them, please"—who seem to believe that God is so disgusted by the sexual activities of homosexuals that he created AIDS to punish them, apparently waiting until 1978 or so to do this, even though homosexual acts have been going on for considerably longer than that, at least since . . . 1956.

I mean, what do they think? God sits around in a lounge chair chatting with Gabriel, planning the fall foliage in Vermont—"I think a lot of orange this year"—when suddenly he says: "Boy oh boy, do I find homosexuals disgusting. I'm going to give them a really horrifying disease!"

And Gabriel says: "Oh yes?"

(*As God:*) Yes! And drug addicts and . . . and . . . hemophiliacs! (*Gabriel looks fairly appalled.*)

(*As Gabriel:*) But why hemophiliacs?

(*God:*) Oh, no reason. I want the disease to go through the bloodstream and even though I'm all-powerful and can do everything 'cause I'm God, I'm too tired today to figure out how to connect the disease to the bloodstream and *not* affect hemophiliacs. Besides, the suffering will be good for them.

(*Gabriel:*) Really? In what way?

(*God:*) Oh, I don't know. I'll explain it at the end of the world.

(*Gabriel:*) I see. Tell me, what about the children of drug addicts? Will they get the disease through their mother's wombs?

(*God:*) Oh, I hadn't thought about that. Well—why not? Serve the hophead mothers right. Boy oh boy, do I hate women drug addicts!

(*Gabriel:*) Yes, but why punish their babies?

(*God:*) And I hate homosexuals!

(*Gabriel:*) Yes, yes, we got you hate homosexuals . . .

(*God:*) Except for Noël Coward; he was droll.

(*Gabriel:*) Yes, he was droll.

(*God:*) And I hate Haitians. Anything beginning with the letter "h."

(*Gabriel:*) Yes, but isn't it unfair to infect innocent babies in the womb with this dreadful disease?

(*God:*) Look, homosexuals and drug addicts are very, very bad people; and if babies get it, well, don't forget I'm God, so you better just presume I have some secret reason why it's good they get it too.

(*Gabriel:*) Yes, but what *is* this secret reason?

(*God:*) Stop asking so many questions.

(*Gabriel:*) Yes, but . . .

(*God:*) There you go again, trying to horn in on the Tree of Knowledge just like Adam and Eve did. Boy oh boy, does that make me wrathful. Okay, Gabriel, you asked for it: I hereby sentence you to become man; I give you suffering and death; I give you psychological pain; I give you AIDS, your immune system will shut down totally, you'll die from brain tumors and diarrhea and horrible random infections. I give you bone cancer, lymph cancer, breast cancer—lots of cancer.

(*A good idea, whimsical.*) Oh! . . . And I hereby revoke penicillin. Anyone out there who has ever been exposed to syphilis will suffer and die just like they used to—as a side issue, I love to connect sex and death, I don't know why I invented sex to begin with, it's a revolting idea, but as long as I have, I want it done *properly*, in the *missionary* position, with *one* person for life, or I want those who disobey me to die a horrible death from AIDS and syphilis and God knows what else. Is that clear???

(*Breaks character and talks to the audience as himself again.*) Now surely that God can't exist—I mean, surely the Christ who said, "Blessed are the merciful" could hardly have come from such a raging, spiteful God. (*Pause, his agitation not quite gone yet. He turns around and stares upstage at the banner for a moment. Turns back to the audience.*)

What *is* that??? (*Looks again. Then back.*)

You know, I don't want to take *away* faith in God from anyone who has it; it's just that I don't follow it. And it's not as if living without a belief in God is so pleasant. In moments of deep despair you have absolutely nothing to fall back on. You just stay in the deep despair for a while, and then if you're lucky, you go to sleep.

But I find more and more that I'm starting to long for some sense of value in things. My mind wanders to reincarnation and karma and karmic paths and so on; in some ways I am turning into Shirley MacLaine. Now one does laugh at her, but I'm starting to really identify with the desire to find some meaning out there.

Because I'm really tired of where I've been. I've been . . . a pretty good "ad-hoc existentialist" for about twenty years. I've gotten up every morning, and I've carried on with my life, acting decent and getting things done, while all the time believing none of it mattered. And I'm really sick of it. I'm *starved* for some meaning. For some belief in something. I'm tired of being an existentialist. It's hard to be joyful when you're an existentialist. Albert Camus was not a laugh riot.

I even went to the Harmonic Convergence ceremony in Central Park this summer. Do you know what I'm referring to? It's this strange, New Age–connected belief, prophesied in several ancient cultures—the Mayan, the Aztec, and the Hopi Indians—that August sixteenth and seventeenth of 1987 represent a window in time in which the planets line up in some special way or other, and that, supposedly, there is an opportunity for mankind to make a spiritual shift away from pollution and destruction of the planet back to being "in alignment" with mother earth, and so on.

The newspapers made fun of the event, and people at the magazine where I work thought I was nuts, but I found I really wanted to believe in this Harmonic Convergence. And even if it was a lot of nonsense, I *liked* the idea of people getting up in the morning all over the world to greet the sunrise and to, if nothing else, sort of hope for a better way of living. I mean, it beats a punch in the eye, doesn't it?

So a couple of friends and I—I'm starting to have more friends who think this way—set our alarms for four in the morning to head up to Eighty-third and Central Park West, which had been designated as a sacred site. (*Realizing that sounds a bit funny.*) Or at least as a place where people were going to gather.

We went over to Sixth Avenue for a taxi and saw all these people getting out of cabs who looked like they were leaving clubs together, going home to have sex, or take cocaine or . . . otherwise give *New York* magazine topics to write on. I guess people still go to clubs. I don't really know anyone who does.

Anyway, predictably we got an absolutely *terrifying* taxi driver. He'd race up to every red light at sixty miles an hour, never slowing down at all just in case the light turned green, which it sometimes did, but you had to worry about the people coming in the other direction who might be trying to run their lights. Anyway, it was harrowing. I kept saying to myself, "All is well in my universe, everyone is calm, no one rushes," but it didn't make him slow down. Finally I had to say, slow down, goddamn it, only I didn't say goddamn it, and he didn't slow down, and eventually we killed two people and a dog. Well, just kidding. But it was a disorienting beginning to the Harmonic Convergence.

Well, in any case, at the sacred site itself, it was very crowded, and there was incense and so on, and wind chimes, and we all sat in a circle. And in the center of the circle there were five women and one man who were blowing on conch shells; and one of the women explained to the crowd that we were all there to align the "horizontal plane" of our present existence with the "vertical plane" of mother earth and the planets or . . . something like that . . . but she seemed a very *warm* woman—she reminded me of someone I know and like named Martha Rhodes. And then the woman said we should all join in and make sounds like the conch shell if we wanted to, and eventually most of the crowd sort of hit this one sustained note that in these circles is described as "toning." (*He takes a moment to breathe and then lets out a low, sustained note, kind of like chanting "ohm." It's just a held note.*) Ahhhhhhhhhhhhhhhhhhhhhhhhhhhhhhhhhhhhhhmmmmmmmmmmmmmmmmm.

I liked doing that. I'm not comfortable meditating yet, but this I could do, and it was nice to be connected to the crowd that way.

And then the sun came up, but the "sacred site chosen" had all these *trees* around it so you couldn't actually *see* the sun. I had almost gone to my friend's roof and part of me wished I were there instead. And then this sort of . . . loopy woman who'd been dancing around the periphery of the circle saying kind of corny things like, "I dance for mother moon and sister star," and stuff like that, and whom I almost admired for having the guts to say things like that, and yet I also thought her sensibility was kind of . . . icky . . . anyway, she got up and invited everyone who wanted to to get up and share their hopes and dreams and prayers for the future. And I realized I didn't want to hear *everyone* in the crowd verbalize their hopes, we'd be stuck for *hours,* listening to a lot of gobbledygook.

And then, of course, the first person to get up to share with the group was one of those mental patients who wander the streets of New York—she looked *demented,* and she was yellow from nicotine, and she talked on and on. And what she said wasn't wrong, exactly—something about why don't people say "I love you" rather than "I hate you"?—but it was upsetting that she was crazy. She reminded me of the woman in the tuna fish aisle, but much more clearly crazy. The woman in the tuna fish aisle could pass for normal on a good day, but this woman really couldn't.

And then the "icky woman" gave the "demented woman" a great big hug in order to *shut her up,* and then some teenager got up to recite a song—not sing it, *recite* it. I don't remember what song it was. Maybe "Blowin' in the Wind." (*Jokes.*) Or "Bali Ha'i." Anyway, it was turning into a nightmare. I didn't want anyone else to speak, I just wanted instant transformation of the planet, and I didn't want to take potluck of listening to any strangers in the crowd say how we should go about it, I didn't trust that they'd know, I just *wanted the transformation.* I didn't want to have to deal with *peo-*

ple about it. And the Harmonic Convergence is about people coming together, and here I was disliking everyone. So I wasn't being very transformed. And my back was sore from sitting—I need to exercise, but I guess I never will—so I asked my friends if we could *please* leave the group and go out into an open area of the park so that we could actually see the sun.

And we did that, and the Great Lawn was very pretty, but I was irritated that we hadn't been there for the actual sunrise.

Well, you can see I was quite resistant, and I did feel bad I was judging everyone there, but then it doesn't really work to pretend you're not feeling something you're feeling. But when you're judging people, you certainly don't feel a sense of unity, do you?

Maybe I shouldn't be so judgmental of people. And it was moving that everyone went there and showed up. I liked that part. And I liked the toning. But otherwise, I felt . . . very separate. (*He looks thoughtful and a little sad at this. He stays in the moment for a bit, and then goes into another affirmation, moving his arms in that circular motion again.*)

I am *not* separate. I am one with the universe. We are all one. We are all part of the same divine energy. (*His tone becomes slightly tongue-in-cheek.*) There are spirit guides above, waiting to guide us. They speak to us through Shirley MacLaine; they knew enough not to choose Shelley Winters. These spirit guides help us. They drive Shirley's car, they make airline reservations for her, they're just great. Bali Ha'i will call you, any night, any day. And they call the wind Maria. (*Pronounced "Ma-rye-a."*) Kumbaya, kumbayae. (*Rhymes with day.*)

Well, now I've depressed myself. But I really am much more positive than I ever used to be, and I think these affirmations are a good thing. It's just that . . . sometimes the bottom drops out for me. And then I need to go sleep for a while and see if tomorrow feels better.

(*Looks around at banner again.*) I wish I knew what that was. It's a great big eye, I see that. I don't know what those things dripping off it are. It looks Egyptian. Or Columbus Avenue. I shouldn't make fun of it. Maybe it is a guide. (*Makes something up.*) It's an "all-seeing eye" that represents inner knowingness, all the wisdom we know from the collective unconscious but, alas, have forgotten. (*He looks over to the crystals and crosses to them.*)

What about crystals? Do you think crystals work? *What works, do you think?* (*He stares at the crystals, wondering what works.*)

Let me try to feel happy again. (*Puts his fingers to his forehead, "flicks" away negativity; pause.*) Let me hold a crystal to my head and try to feel happy. (*Holds the clear crystal to his head; pause; puts the crystal down again.*) Let me give up on feeling happy for now and just concentrate on breathing. (*He inhales audibly, but stops and comes closer to the audience, a little disappointed.*) I don't feel I've helped you very much. But I want you to remember what I said about affirmations. We *can* change our thoughts. And even when we can't, just kinda . . . try to . . . *silence your mind*, and then just breathe. As the last thing between us, let's just breathe, alright? (*He breathes in an exaggerated way, so the audience can get in synch with him. On inhalation he moves his arms up from his diaphragm to his chin; on exhalation, his arms relax downward, the palms open*

in the "receiving" mode. He keeps his eyes closed.) In,
out. In, out. In, out. God, life's monotonous, isn't it? No,
I keep judging things, I'm going to stop doing that. I'm
going to stop talking. Just breathe. *(He returns to his
exaggerated breathing again, this time without words.
Inhale—arms up to chin; exhale—arms down to the
side. He keeps his eyes closed, except on his second full
breath, when he opens them to check how the audience
is doing, breathing with him. On his third breath, he
closes his eyes again, and the lights fade.)*

Dreaming Wild

S C E N E 1

The tuna fish counter in a supermarket.

The MAN *is staring at tuna fish cans, deciding
which one to buy.*

The WOMAN *comes and stands behind him, waiting for him to get out of her way. Her energy is
odd, and she is already overly impatient.*

*He senses her odd energy, kind of half-looks be-
hind him, then decides not to meet her eye—you
shouldn't look at a crazy person—and he starts
studying one particular tuna fish can with intensity, hoping she will go away soon.*

*After a few moments this becomes intolerable for
the* WOMAN *and she raises up her fist and brings*

it down on the Man's head. The MAN *is so thrown off-balance that he falls to the ground.*

WOMAN: Would you kindly move, *asshole!*

(*From off right, the sound of a child crying, as if startled by the Woman's ferocity.*)

MAN: What's the matter with you????

WOMAN: Why didn't you move? I asked you to move!

MAN: No, you didn't!

WOMAN: Yes, I did! (*To offstage, where the crying is coming from:*) Stop crying, little girl, I didn't do anything!

MAN: You're crazy!

(*The* WOMAN *herself starts to cry, and she runs out of the supermarket. The* MAN *stares after her, rubbing his head.*)

Blackout

S C E N E 2

Lights up again on the supermarket aisle.

The MAN *is once again looking at tuna.*

The WOMAN *once again comes in and stands behind him.*

The audience should see that we are replaying the same scene again, so the Man's and Woman's actions should be pretty close to what they were in the previous brief scene.

The Woman's energy is odd, and she is already overly impatient.

He senses her odd energy, decides not to meet her eye, and starts studying one particular tuna fish can with intensity, hoping she will soon go away.

The WOMAN *suddenly speaks with suppressed fury.*

WOMAN (*angry, through clenched teeth, so it's hard to understand her*): You reading a book? I don't have the time!

MAN (*confused; looks at his watch*): Um . . . it's about six-thirty.

WOMAN: That's not what I said, *asshole!* (WOMAN *hits him on the top of the head, he falls. Little girl cries.*) Shut up, little girl! I didn't do anything!

MAN: You're crazy!

(*This time the "You're crazy" remark, rather than making her cry, makes her livid with rage, and she grabs onto the Man's grocery cart. He grabs onto the other end—for protection—and she shakes the cart wildly, sort of growling in rage while she does so. She then runs off again, the* MAN *staring after her.*)

Blackout

S C E N E   3

Lights up again.

The MAN *looking at tuna.*

The WOMAN *comes into the supermarket again, making a beeline for where the* MAN *is standing.*

*Almost before she can get there, the little girl
starts to cry offstage.*

WOMAN (*to crying offstage*): Shut up, little girl, I didn't
do anything yet!

(*The* WOMAN, *irritated and stopped by the little
girl's response, goes offstage again. The* MAN
looks at the WOMAN *very confused, not under-
standing why the little girl cried, or what the*
WOMAN *was talking about. He looks out at the
audience in befuddlement.*)

Blackout

S C E N E 4

Lights up again.

The MAN *looking at tuna.*

The WOMAN *enters and makes a beeline to where
the* MAN *is standing. He senses her energy behind him, looks worried, and holds up a can of
tuna to "study"—but then stops himself and decides on another tack.*

MAN (*polite, reasonable*): Is something the matter?

WOMAN: What?

MAN: Well, you seem . . . odd.

WOMAN (*enraged*): Don't you talk to me that way, *ass-
hole!* (*Hits him on the head; little girl starts crying.*)
Shut up, little girl, I didn't do anything! (*Grabs the
Man's grocery cart and says with glee:*) I'm crazy! (*The*
WOMAN *chases the* MAN *with his own grocery cart. He
runs offstage in terror; she follows in shrieking pursuit.*)

Blackout

S C E N E 5

Lights up again.

The MAN *looking at tuna.*

The WOMAN *enters once again, frustrated per usual.*

The MAN *senses her presence.*

The WOMAN *overcomes her enormous frustration, and asks for what she wants.*

WOMAN: Would you *please* move?

MAN: Are you trying to mug me? (*Turns and aims gun, shoots her dead; the little girl cries offstage.*) Shut up, little girl! (*Aims gun offstage; shoots little girl.*)

Blackout

S C E N E 6

The sound of waves.

Lights up on a blank stage.

The WOMAN *comes downstage in a spot and addresses the audience.*

WOMAN: There's so much violence in my dreams. I've been having this recurring dream about that stupid man in the tuna fish aisle. The other night I dreamed he shot me.

(*The* MAN *comes downstage in another spot and addresses the audience. The* MAN *and the* WO-MAN *are seemingly not aware of one another.*)

MAN: I've been having this recurring dream about the woman in the supermarket. I dream that no matter how else I try to behave, she *always* hits me on the head. The other night, though, I dreamt I shot her. I liked that dream. Although not when I was dreaming it. It was upsetting then. (*The* MAN *freezes during the Woman's next speech.*)

WOMAN: I dreamt I was back at Creedmoor, and one of the orderlies was saying to me, "The universe doesn't make sense, there is no order, you should be a star like Edie Sedgwick, but you're not." And then I was in the institution dining room, and all the other people at the table were being really disgusting with their food, so I didn't want to look at this, so I kept staring at my plate. And on my plate there was this baked potato. And I started to get really afraid of this baked potato, and so finally I took my knife and fork to open it up and inside the baked potato was my father—who I didn't know very well, he left my mother and me when I was pretty young. And so I wanted to know how he was, but when I asked him he said, "Who are you, I don't know you." So I put butter on him and ate him. (*The* WOMAN *freezes during the Man's next speech.*)

MAN: The other night I dreamt my father was inside a baked potato. Isn't that strange? I was very startled to see him there, and I started to be afraid other people would see where my father was, and how small he was, so I kept trying to close the baked potato, but I guess the potato was hot, 'cause he'd start to cry when I'd shut the baked potato, so then I didn't know what to do. I thought of sending the whole plate back to the kitchen—tell the cook there's a person in my baked potato—but then I felt such guilt at deserting my father that I just sat there at the table and cried. He cried too. Then the waiter brought dessert, which was devil's food cake with mocha icing, and I ate that. Then I woke up, very hungry. I told my therapist about the dream, and he said that the baked potato represented either the womb or where I tried to put my father during the Oedipal conflict—"What Oedipal conflict?" I always say to him, "I won, hands down." And then my therapist said my father cried because he was unhappy, and that I dreamt about the cake because I was hungry. I think my therapist is an idiot. Maybe I should just have gurus. Or find a nutritionist. But what I'm doing now isn't working.

(*Lights off the* MAN. *The* WOMAN *is alone onstage.*)

WOMAN: And then the night after my baked potato dream, I dreamt about that stupid man from the tuna fish aisle again, and in my dream I got so mad at him that I started to feel sorry for myself, but then Nazis started to chase me and I had to hide in the frozen foods counter. And then the next night I dreamt that I killed Sally Jessy Raphael.

MAN (*from offstage*): And now the Sally Jessy Raphael Show.

(*The stage is transformed into a talk-show setting, a kind of crackpot "dream" talk show, mixing up the supermarket and the TV show. The* WOMAN *discovers a microphone and red-framed glasses [similar to those worn by the real Sally Jessy Raphael], which she puts on.*)

WOMAN: Hello. Sally Jessy Raphael can't be here today because I killed her. My aggression finally got the better of me, but what can you expect living in New York? These *are* her red-framed glasses, however. Do you like me in them? Now when my eyes are bloodshot from weeping or from allergies, you won't be able to tell whether it's my eyes that are red or my glasses!

This isn't my first time before the camera you know. The late Andy Warhol discovered me, and he said I should be as famous as Edie Sedgwick. That isn't very famous, of course, but those of you who follow the East Village scene and take drugs know who I mean. Ahahahahahahahahaha.

I hope you don't mind if I do that, but I'm hoping to make that my signature on the air rather than these fuckin' glasses. Ahahahaha.

Let's see. Sally Jessy Raphael used to say "troops" a lot, I'll try that. Hey, troops! How are you? Do you like my glasses? That way when my eyes are red, you can't tell if I've been crying or someone's punched me! Ahahahaha. Did I tell you about my father in the baked potato? I ate him. Now, troops, I don't mean sexually, I mean I ate him cannibalistically. Ahahahaha. Just kidding about that, troops, but know that my pain is sincere.

However, our show today isn't about cannibalism and it isn't about oral sex, although Dr. Ruth *is* a friend of mine . . . That's a lie, I hate Dr. Ruth and I hate Mother Theresa! I want them to fight to the death with chains and nuclear-fueled revolving dildos! I'm sorry (*calls out to technicians in the distance or offstage*) . . . can I say the word "dildo" on television? What? Read off the cards? Read off what cards? (*Sees something, reads from it.)* A E I O U. *(Tries to pronounce it.)* Aeiou? Well, that's an eye chart, not an idiot card. No, these cards are not useful. I am not an optimist. No, that's a slip of the tongue. I am not an optometrist. I am a talk-show host or hostess.

Today our show is about nuclear proliferation. *And* it's also about the destruction of the ozone layer. *And* it's about sex education in the schools—should we tell our children about condoms or just wait until they get AIDS? And it's about AIDS, and it's about society's views on homosexuality—is it disgusting or is it delightful? And it's about the electoral college in our voting system—should we change it, should we rethink it, should we charge the delegates to the electoral college a tuition fee? And it's about free speech versus pay speech. Should people be allowed to say what they think? Should we demand that people who talk more pay more taxes? And it's about President Reagan and taxes. Does he know what he's talking about, or is he already dead? Anyway, it's about all these topics—nuclear proliferation, condoms and children, the ozone layer, AIDS, homosexuality, heterosexuality, free speech, necrophilia and the presidency, and changing the electoral college—*and* we have to cover all these topics in under thirty minutes! So I better stop talking and bring out my first guest. Won't you join me in welcoming the Infant of Prague?

(Enter the MAN *dressed as the Infant of Prague. Now what do I mean by this? The Infant of Prague is a seventeenth-century artist's invention of what the Christ Child, triumphant, might look like: Catholics are familiar with the look of this—usually in Infant of Prague statues—found in their churches, or sometimes on dashboards.*

Non-Catholics usually have not heard of the In-
fant of Prague, but some may recognize the look:
a golden-haired child (of about ten to twelve
maybe), dressed ornately. The most common
look has white robes, embroidered with pearls
and jewels, covered with a bright red cape, with
white ruffles at the neck and wrists. On the top of
the child's golden curls is a great big whopping
crown, of gold and red, not unlike the crown in
Imperial Margarine commercials on TV; that is,
it's big and has the "ball-like" red thing at the top
of it. The Infant, in his left hand, always carries a
large orb, usually blue and with a gold cross on
top of it, and always has his right hand raised,
with his first two fingers held upright and his
thumb and other two fingers folded in on one
another. Since the Infant of Prague is usually a
statue, or sometimes a large doll, the costume
resembles a statue rather than a person, or an
enormous, walking chess piece. The Infant's per-
sonality, by the way, is sunny and beatifically
unflappable.)

WOMAN (*to herself*): Why am I dreaming about the Infant of Prague? I don't even know what that is.

MAN (*to audience; not in character as the Infant, and*
perhaps lowering his upraised right hand): I dreamt I
was the Infant of Prague appearing on the Sally Jessy
Raphael show, though I've never even heard of her. (*The*
MAN *raises his right hand, with its two upraised fin-*
gers, and resumes being the Infant.)

WOMAN: Infant of Prague, won't you sit down?

MAN: Thank you, Sally, I only stand.

WOMAN: I'm not Sally. Sally is dead.

MAN (*with sympathy*): Oh. And is she in heaven with my father?

WOMAN: I really don't know. Enough chitchat. Tell me—"Infant of Prague"—is that your first name?

MAN: My name is the Infant of Prague, and I am a representation of the Christ Child.

WOMAN: Really. Where do you live?

MAN: I am housed in the Church of Our Lady of Victory in Prague, capital of Czechoslovakia.

WOMAN (*penetratingly*): Where is Prague exactly?

MAN: It's in Czechoslovakia.

WOMAN: And where is Czechoslovakia?

MAN (*confused*): It's in Prague.

WOMAN: Ahahahahahahaha! (*To Infant:*) That's my signature. Do you like my glasses? They're red. That way you can't tell if roving street gangs beat me up or not.

MAN: What?

WOMAN: Never mind. Tell us, Infant, a little bit about yourself.

> (*The Infant addresses a lot of his comments directly and happily to the audience because he is a born teacher and because he is divine.*)

MAN: A statue of me was given to the Discalced Carmelites in Prague in 1628 by Princess Polyxena Lobkowitz.

WOMAN: Polly who Lobka-what?

MAN: The statue was a gift from her mother, Maria Mariquez de Lara, who had brought the statue with her to Bohemia when she married the Czech nobleman, Vratsilav of Pernstyn.

WOMAN: Princeton? Princeton, New Jersey?

MAN: No, not Princeton. *Pern*-styn.

WOMAN: Uh huh. I wonder if I have any other guests that could come on. (*Calls offstage.*) Oh, Ed? Is there anybody back there? (*To herself:*) Who's Ed? I don't know any Ed. Oh never mind. (*To Infant:*) Tell us, Infant, a little about what you're wearing. (*To audience:*) That's pretty wild, isn't it troops?

MAN: I'm glad you asked me that, Sally.

WOMAN: I'm not Sally. Sally's dead.

MAN: Then she's in heaven with my father. My inner garments are similar to the priest's alb, and are made of white linen and of lace. (*Proudly shows a bit of his undergarments, or beneath a ruffle.*)

WOMAN: Ooooh, this is getting racy.

MAN: Please don't make sacrilegious remarks or I'll have to leave.

WOMAN: I always get the difficult guests. First Eartha Kitt, and now a tea cozy.

MAN (*turning as in a fashion show*): Covering my inner garments is a miniature liturgical cope, made of heavy damask, richly woven with gold and embroidered with pearls.

(The WOMAN *may go out into the audience to ask her questions.)*

WOMAN: Wow, you could really feed a lot of starving people with that outfit there, couldn't you, Infant?

MAN *(firmly)*: Most people do not eat gold and pearls, Sally.

WOMAN: Sally's dead, how many times do I have to tell you that!

MAN: Three times, representing the Blessed Trinity. Father, Son, and Holy Spirit.

WOMAN *(referring to the orb)*: What's that little paperweight in your hand?

MAN: This is not a paperweight. It is a miniature globe, signifying the worldwide kingship of the Christ Child.

WOMAN: Uh huh. Well, fine, let's move on, shall we? *(A glint in her eye.)* Let's talk about condoms for a bit. Your church isn't very big on condoms, is it?

MAN: When people ask me, the Infant of Prague, for advice on sexuality, I sometimes think to myself, what do I know about sex?—I'm an infant. What's more, I'm the Infant of Prague; I can't sit down, let alone have sex. *(Laughs good-naturedly at his quip.)* But what people don't realize sometimes is that God my father has a holy and blessed purpose to the mystery of sexuality, and that purpose is to create other little infants like myself to glorify God and creation. That is why condoms are wrong, because anything that intercepts—or *contra*-cepts—this process is deeply wrong.

WOMAN: Now let's get real here for a second, Infant. People are always going to have sex, and now we have this deadly disease AIDS which is killing people, and one of the ways to protect oneself is to use a condom. Now don't you think we better get *practical* here, and get people to use condoms? Whaddya say, Infant of Prague???

MAN: We must instruct the people at risk to abstain from sex.

WOMAN: Oh, well, fine. And we can tell the waterfall to stop falling, but is that practical?

MAN: Moses parted the Red Sea. (*Smiles at the audience, having made an unassailable point.*)

WOMAN: Uh huh. So let's get this straight—you would prefer that adolescents die from AIDS rather than tell them about condoms?

MAN: I do not prefer this at all, Sally. Yes, I know, Sally is dead. Sorry, I keep forgetting. Sally, I would tell all the teenagers of the world to be like me, an infant without sexual urges, until they were much, much older and ready to commit to one person for life, and to glory in the sacramental beauty of sex, within marriage, where during the actual act of intercourse all you can think about is "Procreation! Procreation! I am going to have a little baby, a little infant to glorify God!"

WOMAN: Well, the teenagers in New Jersey are gonna love that answer. *Come on, Infant.* Don't you think you're a *little* impractical.

MAN: The Divine *is* impractical, that's why it's divine.

(*The Infant smiles delightedly, another unassailable point. The* WOMAN *would like to kill him.*)

WOMAN (*to audience*): We have to take a little break here, but we'll be right back with more of the Infant of Prague. (ON-THE-AIR *sign goes off, and theme music starts. Off the air, the* WOMAN *unleashes her pent-up fury and begins to pummel the Infant.*) YOU JERK, YOU STUBBORN SHIT, YOU EFFEMINATE EU-NUCH, YOU MAKE ME WANT TO VOMIT WITH YOUR HOLIER-THAN-THOU ATTITUDE! WHY SHOULD WE LISTEN TO YOU ABOUT SEX??? YOU'RE AFRAID OF SEX, YOUR IDEAS ON SEX ARE RIGID AND INSANE, AND SOMEONE SHOULD HAVE YOU KILLED! I WANT YOU *DEAD!* DIE, DIE, DIE!

(*The Infant looks startled and alarmed during this outburst. Toward the end of her outburst, one of her hits makes him fall over backwards, and the* WOMAN *dives on top of him, continuing her pummeling. The* ON-THE-AIR *sign comes back on, as does the theme music. The* WOMAN *looks out, caught in the act of straddling and beating up her guest. She gets off of him and talks to the camera. The Infant remains on the ground, un-able to stand up due to the weight of his clothes and crown. He struggles from time to time, mov-ing his slippered feet about pathetically.*)

Well, we're back on the air now. Ahahahahaha. Let's *talk* about "air," and the ozone layer, shall we? (*Notices the Infant's struggling, explains to the camera.*) He fell down during the commercial.

MAN: Would you help me stand up please?

WOMAN: Wait a minute. Give me your opinion on the destruction of the ozone layer.

MAN: I am opposed to the destruction of the ozone layer, Sally.

WOMAN: Who did we tell you was dead?

MAN: Sally.

WOMAN: Right answer. Alright, I'll help you up now. (*The* WOMAN *helps the Infant stand up. He looks disoriented for a moment.*) Okay. Let's go for the "gold." What about homosexuality—is it disgusting or is it delightful?

MAN: It is a grievous sin. But I love homosexuals, I just want them to be celibate until they die.

WOMAN: Who booked this jerk on here anyway??? (*Calls offstage again.*) Ed, I'm talking to you!

MAN: Where is Sally?

WOMAN: Who is Ed?

MAN: I don't want to be interviewed by you anymore. (*Starts to wander offstage and to call out.*) Sally? Sally!

WOMAN (*takes out a gun and aims it at him*): I killed Sally Jessy Raphael, and I can kill you! (*Shoots him several times.*)

MAN: It is not possible to kill the Infant of Prague. (*He exits happily. She is enraged.*)

WOMAN (*calling off after him*): I hate you, I hate you, you Infant of Prague! (*To audience:*) I hate religious bigots. And I hate people who think they know what's right. And I hate people who are filled with hate. And I hate people who are filled with love. I wish my mother had had me killed when I was a fetus. That's the kind of person I am. Do you get it? Ahahahahahaha!

WOMAN'S VOICE (*on tape*): My next guest today is Rama Sham Rama.

WOMAN: I don't want no fucking next guest! (*Shoots her gun offstage, apparently stopping Rama Sham Rama; then calls off in the other direction.*) Ed!! You're fired! (*Shoots her gun off in Ed's direction. The theme music plays nightmarishly, and the talk-show set disappears or recedes into the distance. The* WOMAN *is now back in her waking-dream state again, and addresses the audience as herself once more, out of her Sally dream.*) Why is there so much violence in my dreams? I'm always killing people or they're killing me. The other night I dreamt I killed Sally Jessy Raphael. And then I tried to kill the Infant of Prague, whoever the hell that is. Then Rama Sha Rambus somebody. I have to let go of this rage, I can't live this way anymore.

(*Lights off the* WOMAN, *spot on the* MAN, *dressed back in his normal clothes again.*)

MAN: I dreamt the other night that I was in Central Park before dawn at the Harmonic Convergence ceremony, and that the icky woman was talking about her hopes for mankind again, but that various mental patients kept interrupting her.

(*Lights back on the* WOMAN. *The Man's spot stays on also, though he doesn't yet hear what she's saying.*)

WOMAN: I dreamt that I was at the Harmonic Convergence—whatever the hell that is. Something is wrong with my dreams lately, I keep dreaming about things I've never heard about. Anyway, and this woman with a flower in her head kept saying things like "I dance for the sun king," and "I dance for the moon king"—it made me *real* hostile. So I called out at the top of my lungs, "Why don't you get your tooth fixed?"

MAN: Oh! And then I dreamt that the woman from the tuna fish aisle was there, and she shouted at the icky woman, "Why don't you see a dentist?" or, "There's something wrong with your tooth," or something like that. But it didn't make much sense, there wasn't anything wrong with the woman's tooth.

WOMAN: And then all these aging hippies were sitting with their legs crossed and their eyes closed, doing meditation . . . (*The* MAN *closes his eyes and puts his arms at his sides, palms out, joining in the meditation.*) . . . and I yelled out, "WHAT DO YOU THINK THIS IS— 1967???" And then someone gave me a flower, and I said, "Oh, fuck you!" and I ripped the flower up, and they had this real hurt look on their face, and then everyone started to make sounds together . . .

MAN (*toning, a low, calm sound*): Ohhhhhhhhhhhhhh-mmmmmmmmmmmmmmmm . . . (*Continues toning.*)

WOMAN: Ohhhhhhhhhhhmmmmmmmmmmmmmmm. So then I did that for a while. But I got bored, so I thought, I know, I'll pretend to be a car alarm, so I went: eeeeeeeeeeeeeeeEEEEEEEEEEEEEEEEEEEEEEEEEEEEEE-EEEEEEEEEEEEEEEEEEEEEEEEEEEEEEE . . .

(*The* WOMAN *does an upsettingly successful imitation of a shrieking car alarm. The* MAN *seems*

to hear it in his unconscious, and it fights with
his "ohm" sound. He frowns.)

MAN (*continuing through above*): ... mmmmmmm-
mmmmmmmmmmmm. Then I turned *off* my alarm
... (*Makes a gesture of turning off alarm; the* WOMAN
stops making her noise.) ... which was waking me, but
then I went right back to sleep, and now the icky
woman wasn't there anymore, and somehow I had been
designated the person who was supposed to run the
ceremony in her absence. I tried to blow on a conch
shell, which I thought I had in my hand, but it was
actually a ham sandwich, so, of course, when I blew on
it, it didn't make any noise. So then I addressed the
crowd.

(*Lights shift. The* MAN *crosses center. The sound*
of a light wind, and of tinkling wind chimes. The
WOMAN *is seated nearby. He and she are now in a*
kind of joint dream about the Harmonic Conver-
gence. The setting is a dreamlike setting of Cen-
tral Park, with bushes and shrubbery around,
mixed in strangely with parts of the supermarket
aisle and some of the elements of the talk show as
well. It is lit like night, a bit before dawn. The
MAN *speaks to the crowd, projecting a bit loudly.*)

I seem to have misplaced my conch shell. If anyone
finds it, please let me know.

WOMAN (*disruptively loud*): WHAT THE FUCK'S A
CONCH SHELL?

MAN (*trying to pay no attention*): I have been asked to
lead the ceremony until dawn comes. The icky
woman—that is ... Vicki, her name is Vicki—has had to

leave the park to take several patients back to various mental institutions.

WOMAN: Was any of them Creedmoor? I have connections at Creedmoor.

MAN (*to* WOMAN, *patiently, but bothered*): Please, don't just call out, I find it disorienting.

WOMAN: Why don't you get your tooth fixed?

MAN: There is nothing wrong with my tooth. (*To crowd:*) We are here to enter a new age. The planets of Mars and . . . Hathor are in alignment with the seventh moon of the seventh sun of the seventh seal.

WOMAN: Why don't you give me a job?

MAN: Please everyone hold a crystal to your head and align yourself with mother earth. (*Holds a small clear crystal to his head and closes his eyes to concentrate.*)

WOMAN: If you hire me at the magazine, I promise not to write "pig" on the wall with your blood!

MAN: I would not be willing to hire you under those circumstances.

WOMAN: Well, fuck you!

MAN: Can someone take this woman away? Is Vicki back?

WOMAN: Vicki's dead. She and Mother Theresa fought to the death with knives at the coliseum.

MAN (*closes his eyes, does his affirmation hands-in-a-circular-motion gestures*): Everyone in my universe is cooperative. I am a natural leader, and no one yells out in the middle of my speaking. I let the gems of the earth empower me. (*Holds the crystal to his forehead.*)

WOMAN: Why are you holding that piece of chandelier to your forehead?

MAN: It's a crystal.

WOMAN: And my doctors think *I'm* crazy.

MAN: Would you please be quiet?

WOMAN: No! (*Sings the same light and pretty song she sang at beginning of play, only now sings operatically, to annoy the MAN and to block out what he's saying.*)

MAN (*trying to ignore her*): The earth is entering a *new phase* where it is going to evaluate what man has done to it over the past many centuries. And, if there are one hundred and forty-four thousand *enlightened people* on the earth at the time of the Harmonic Convergence, it's possible we can shift away from death and destruction . . .

WOMAN: I dance for the sun king! (*Dances across the stage in a put-on, arty way.*)

MAN: . . . to a place of unity, and unconditional love and harmony . . .

WOMAN: I dance for the moon king! (*Dances some more.*)

MAN: . . . both for mankind and for the planet.

WOMAN: And when I don't dance, I laugh. Ahahahahah-ahahaha!

MAN: We only have a few minutes left until dawn.

WOMAN (*suddenly direct, to the* MAN): You're blocking my way.

MAN: We should all be silent now, until the dawn.

WOMAN: You're blocking my way.

MAN: What?

WOMAN: Why are you always blocking my way to the tuna fish?

MAN: What tuna fish? There isn't any tuna fish here. We're in Central Park.

WOMAN: Well, what's that then?

> (*She points upstage where, indeed, there is a section of supermarket aisle with tuna fish cans on it, mixed in with the Central Park shrubbery. The* MAN *is very disoriented. There had been no tuna fish in his Central Park dream up till now.*)

MAN (*very annoyed, to the crowd*): Why is there tuna fish in Central Park??

WOMAN: It's a Gristedes. It's very convenient.

MAN: No, we all have to cooperate now, this isn't the time for tuna fish.

WOMAN: I want to get by you!

MAN: No, we have to prepare for the dawn.

WOMAN: I make the dawn come up like thunder!

MAN: No! Now go sit down and wait. Can't you do that?

WOMAN: I'm always being told to wait. When is it my turn??

MAN: NEVER! NOW SIT THE FUCK DOWN!!!

(*The* WOMAN *is startled by the Man's fury. She sits. He begins to tone, somewhat abruptly, after his screaming.*)

Ohhhhhhhhhhhhhhmmmmmmmmmmmmmmmm . . .

WOMAN (*hands covering ears, hating the sound*): Stop making that noise!

(*The* MAN *continues to tone. The* WOMAN *is driven crazy by the sound. She stands and makes her car alarm sound again. She crosses to him, dreamlike, raises her fist in slow motion, and brings it down on his head. He falls to the ground, and she is now free to get to the tuna fish finally. All sound stops. The* WOMAN *runs over to the tuna fish aisle, thrilled.*)

At last! I'm here now, I'm safe, I'm here, I have what I want! (*Takes a can, reads it.*) Poison. (*Throws it offstage, looks at next one.*) Poison. (*Throws it offstage, looks at next one.*) Poison! (*Throws it, looks at next one.*) Salmon. I don't want salmon. (*Throws it, looks at next one.*) Poison! (*Throws it, looks at next one.*) To-mato soup! (*Throws it.*) WHAT IS THE MATTER WITH THIS STORE??? (*Weeps. The* WOMAN *moves away from the aisle. The stage darkens.*)

MAN (*starts to come to from having been hit, rubs his head, and notices the darkening around him*): Oh, ev-erything's turning black. Keep toning. Ohhhhhhhh-hhhhhhhhhhhhhhhmmmmmmmmmm . . .

(*The Woman's weeping continues. The sound of the little girl crying offstage is heard also, night-*

marishly. The MAN *keeps trying to tone, to drown out the sound of crying.*)

If people are going to refuse to tone, the dawn may not come up. Ohhhhhhhhhhhhhhhmmmmmmmmm. Ohhhhhhhhhhhhmmmmmmm. (*To weeping* WOMAN:) SHUT UP! (*The lights shift to two spotlights, one on the* MAN, *one on the* WOMAN. *All noise stops.*)

WOMAN (*to audience*): And then I dreamt that the man in the tuna fish aisle was suddenly empathetic with me.

MAN (*to audience*): And then I dreamt that the woman and I were still in Central Park and she was still weeping, but I felt this sudden wave of empathy for her.

(*The lights shift back to how they were before the asides. The* WOMAN *goes back to weeping, but the scene is otherwise quiet. The* MAN *tries to think how to speak to her.*)

What's the matter?

WOMAN: I'm laughing wild amid severest woe.

MAN: But you're weeping.

WOMAN: Oh, sorry. (*Burst of crazy laughter.*) Ahah-ahahahahahahahaha!

MAN: Did you get the tuna fish you need?

WOMAN: Why don't you get your tooth fixed?

MAN: Ummmm ... That's a good suggestion, thank you, I will.

WOMAN: The tuna fish is all mislabeled. Some of it is salmon, and some of it is poison, and some of it is tomato soup.

MAN: That's a shame. Maybe you would like to tell the people here in the park about your hopes for the Harmonic Convergence?

WOMAN: Yes, I would. (*Addresses the crowd, with a soft quality.*) I hope that the pounding in my head stops. And I hope that people will not spit on me as I pass them in the street. And I hope that someone gives me a job. And I hope that I have more good days than bad days. That I learn to say this glass is half full, it is not half empty. And to hell with my half-full glass—I want a *full* full glass, I want it overflowing. And I want to feel joy like I did that one summer day for ten minutes right before I decided life was horrible and I went crazy. I want to recapture the feeling of *liking* to be alive. I want to feel joy that looks like this.

> (*She throws her head back and spreads her arms wide in an exuberant, open, receiving position. The darkness on the stage changes to vibrant color: deep purple to deep red to a warm, rose hue. In other words, it's dawn, though not presented realistically. The MAN notices the light. He stands and feels he should probably continue leading the crowd.*)

MAN: Everybody breathe. In . . .

> (*The WOMAN is in her exuberant, head-thrown-back posture still. Without making it a big deal, she automatically joins the Man's, and crowd's, breathing rhythms.*)

WOMAN: And out . . .

> (*The MAN notes her joining. Again, no big deal, but it's the first time they've had agreement on anything ever. There is relief. Breathing, dawn.*)

MAN: In . . .

WOMAN: . . . and out . . .

> (*The* MAN *and the* WOMAN *maybe look at one another on their last lines, before the lights fade.*)

MAN: In . . .

WOMAN: . . . and out . . .

Afterword: Laughing Wild

Eggs, butter, cheese. Return phone calls to Jon Denny, Jay Siem at Merrill Lynch, Nancy Quinn at the Young Playwrights Festival. Answer letter from three years ago asking me to speak on "Whither American Drama" at the University of Rochester. Buy triple-A batteries for my VCR remote control.

I went to a restaurant the other day and read David Mamet's *Writing in Restaurants*. I ordered eggs benedict and spilled hollandaise sauce on the book, purposely. When I give in to it, I have a lot of free-floating hostility floating around, and yet I feel I am a kind person.

Last year I was reexperiencing my feelings of grief and deep sorrow at feeling (or being) abandoned at the age of three, when my mother went into a deep depression at the death of her second child and my father was stopping up his feelings by drinking. This year I am about to relive parts of my adolescence. Along these lines, I have grown my first beard; it has bits of gray in it, which is not appropriate for a teenager but is fine for a man of my age.

Some days I want to kill Frank Rich, the drama critic of *The New York Times*. He represents this Great Deaf Ear I must somehow get through to in order to reach a theatre-going public. The "New Age" part of me knows this perception regarding him is merely a giving away of my power to him, and, truthfully, in New York I seem to have an audience that comes to my plays regardless, more or less, of what he says.

The genuine problem I face is that the approval and hoopla of the *Times* is very important to creating an "atmosphere" around a play, a sense that one should see it soon, and this "must see" quality is what sells tickets at the beginning and motivates a producer to move a play from a nonprofit New York theatre (like Play-wrights Horizons or Manhattan Theatre Club) to a commercial run on or off Broadway. After a couple of months, this *Times* support is much less important, and then word of mouth kicks in. But for that initial period, the *Times* support is awfully significant. And having your play in an open commercial run—versus a few weeks at a nonprofit theatre—is of enormous differ-ence in terms of reaching a larger audience, and of fi-nances. (You can make a living with royalties from a play that runs; you can pay maybe two months' rent with payment from a play at a nonprofit theatre.)

Oh Lord, I really don't want to talk about the critics particularly, because I don't see a solution in sight, and yet every time I sit down to work on the notes for this play the issue comes charging up for me.

Everyone in theatre knows how crazy it is to have One Critical Voice that carries such weight, and that it's the result of having only one newspaper that most of the theatre-going public seems to read. It's pointless to blame anyone because nobody "caused" this state of affairs. But most people in theatre suffer severely under this state of affairs.

Nothing similar exists in movies or books because they are reviewed nationally, and quickly a consensus forms. For instance, Woody Allen's film *Hannah and Her Sisters* received a very ho-hum response from Pauline

Kael in *The New Yorker*. The bulk of the other reviews indicated a consensus that *Hannah* was one of his best films, and Kael's opinion quickly fit into its proper place as an idiosyncratic nay vote. If *Hannah* had been a play and the gifted Ms. Kael had been the *New York Times* theatre critic, *Hannah* would probably have closed.

The truth is, I'm worn out working in this system. Of my last four plays—*Beyond Therapy, Baby with the Bathwater, The Marriage of Bette and Boo*, and *Laughing Wild*—the *Times* (in the pontifical voice of Rich) only liked *Baby with the Bathwater*, and that, due to his review, was the one that came closest to being moved to a commercial run. However, it was the one that least should have been considered for a commercial run since audiences *way* preferred the other three, especially *Beyond Therapy*, which most people found very funny, and *Bette and Boo*, which most found funny and touching.

Twice now I've had ecstatic receptions to plays on opening nights—*Bette and Boo* and *Laughing Wild*— that are impossible for me to enjoy because I know I'm waiting for the word from His Lord Chief Executioner. It's such a stupid system. If he didn't write for the major newspaper in New York, Frank Rich's opinion per se would be of zero interest to me, especially as the years have gone on and he's gotten harder and harder and harder. It must be all that veal he eats at Orso's.

Now, one can buck the system to a point. If a producer is aggressive and pours money into a campaign and gets the actors to take lower salaries and gets the writer, director, and designers to waive their royalties (and everyone is getting low salaries to begin with), you can keep a show open until it finds its audience. Jack Mc-Quiggen, producer of Larry Shue's *The Foreigner*, did that in recent years. So did the producers of Shue's *The Nerd*. More power to those people.

In my situation I've mostly been working with the New York nonprofit theatres that have subscription seasons of plays so that a play either must be so acclaimed that it moves to a different theatre (a commercial house on or off Broadway) or must close to make room for the next play. So, in those houses—Playwrights Horizons, Manhattan Theatre Club, the Public Theatre (though Joe Papp has a bit more flexibility, having more spaces)—one cannot keep a play running open ended until an audience "finds" it. One must be acclaimed, with the accompanying hoopla causing a flurry of box office activity that pretty much demands a move to a commercial run—which is, indeed, what happened with my play *Sister Mary Ignatius Explains It All For You* at Playwrights Horizons in 1981. Without the critical *Times* hoopla, you most likely will close in a few weeks to make room for the next play.

Now, in a "this glass is half-full, not half-empty" scenario, I must admit I get my plays produced—even abroad—and I make a living. So what more do I want?

Well, the truth is, I do want more. I want to work in a theatrical arena where one man's opinion does not carry this crazy weight, where if audiences and other critics find *Beyond Therapy* funny, Mr. Rich's opinion that it is not funny will not count except as a tiny part of a larger consensus. But seemingly I can't have that. The *Times* is totally unmoving about "taking responsibility" for its power. People from the theatre community have been meeting with its editors on and off for at least twenty years, and the *Times* prides itself on being open to solving this problem and claims to be embarrassed by its power. But the possible solutions to the problem—having more than one critic review a play at a time, running a "scorecard" of what the other critics said, even a tiny suggestion like having "opinion" writ-

ten at the top of the review—are invariably overruled by
the *Times*. The truth is, whether they admit it to themselves or not, the editors of the *Times* and Rich love
their power. It makes them feel, well, powerful.

So, in truth, to overcome Frank Rich I have either to
work with more aggressive producers (like the afore-
mentioned McQuiggen, who bucked the critical rejec-
tion of *The Foreigner* to keep it running until audiences
found it, thereby making his property very valuable and
produced all over the country), or somehow to be satis-
fied with a four-week-run at a nonprofit theatre in New
York.

But I feel worn out by the notion. I don't want to go up
in front of His Pontiff Rich again. Theatre seems an
unfriendly and unaccepting arena to work in, at least in
New York. I can't seem to see around this problem right
now. I've recently had good times writing for camcra—a
half-hour episode of PBS' *Trying Times* series called
"The Visit" starring Swoosie Kurtz, and a crackpot
seven-minute film for Showtime's *By-line* series that
was a mock documentary of my life as a writer (with
Christine Estabrook as my wife who sleeps on the
kitchen floor). It was fun to make these works, and to
know there was no one-man pit bull waiting to devour
them. Maybe it's time to hand the theatre over to Rich—
let him order it just like his veal and pasta at Orso's.

I love theatre, which is why there's anger (and sorrow)
in my tone for what I perceive Rich and the *Times* to
have done to New York theatre, and to my possible
place in it. It's just not a good place here.

Afterword:
Baby With the Bathwater

I wrote the afterword to *Laughing Wild* nearly nine months ago. I have nothing new to add to it, or take away from it, but wanted to talk a bit about the two plays in this volume.

I wrote the first act of *Baby with the Bathwater* as a self-contained one-act sometime in late 1981. Then in late 1982 Robert Brustein, whom I knew from my days as a student at Yale Student of Drama (where he had been dean), told me he wanted to do the one-act *Baby* at his American Repertory Theatre in Cambridge, Massachusetts on a double bill with a Beckett one-act. I had been toying with the notion of expanding *Baby*, wondering what would happen if I followed subsequent years in *Baby's* life, so I asked Brustein if he'd be interested in doing a full-length *Baby with the Bathwater*, were I to come up with one. He said yes.

He then went on to schedule the full-length version before I had written it, which flattered me. However, when I heard the due dates, I became momentarily alarmed—I had to write Act Two in six weeks or something in order to be ready for the scheduled first rehearsal. That wasn't much time, and what if I got stuck in the writing?

But then I shifted back to being flattered by his faith in me and what I'd come up with, and I also knew that in many instances I could (and did) write very, very fast. So I decided just to accept the shortness of time, and write quickly.

I had a really good time writing Act Two and think it's clearly better than Act One (which makes the play, I'm afraid, a bit lopsided in performance).

Act One was written in a bit of a throwback to the absurdist style of my first plays (*Nature and Purpose of the Universe, Titanic, 'dentity Crisis*)—a style not unlike that of Ionesco, or Edward Albee's *The American Dream. Sister Mary Ignatius Explains It All for You* and *Beyond Therapy,* the two plays that preceded this one, had their own comic exaggerations (especially the end of *Sister*), but they both had a kind of reality going— Sister, for instance, walks to her lectern, she doesn't pop out of a big box the way Nanny does; Bruce in *Beyond Therapy* may cry unexpectedly but he doesn't, say, show psychological upset by crouching next to the refrigerator or lying in a pile of laundry the way John and Daisy do in *Bathwater.*

Act Two skips through time as we follow the child Daisy's growth without ever seeing him. I enjoyed bringing back the absurdist details of Act One in semi-realistic form in Act Two: having the child Daisy write an essay, for instance, in which the infant's fear of the German shepherd, and of buses, and of being called a baked potato, all come back to haunt him. I also got an enormous kick out of writing the Woman Principal in that essay scene, and kept laughing out loud as I wrote her.

Then I liked switching tone in Daisy's monologue, where we realize that (a) he's male, not female; and (b) for all the absurdist trappings, he's in a lot of pain. Taking Daisy's pain (and for that matter, his parents' pain) seriously at the same time that I expect the audience to find humor in it has become for me the definition of my style, or at least what I intend it to be: absurdist comedy married to real feelings.

The ending of the play was, for me, my first genuinely "hopeful" ending. I had been criticized for not ending my plays well, and most of the previous plays had what I call "dot dot dot" (. . .) endings, in which the audience sees the characters once more doing the same damn thing they've been doing all their lives, and now sees they're just going to keep on doing it forever, as the lights dim (. . .).

It's the opposite of plays in which characters change; the whole point of these endings tends to be that people *don't* change. I felt there was no intrinsic reason why endings *had* to have big character changes or big revelations that huff and puff, trying to explain everything. The challenge, though, with the (. . .) ending is to restate the problem in a way that is dramatically satisfying and amusing to an audience (such as, I think, the sex-change couple mock-explaining the play's meaning in *'dentity Crisis* and then conjugating the word "identity": I dentity, you dentity, he, she, or it . . . etc.).

When I approached the ending of *Bathwater*, I surprised myself by not wanting to show Daisy repeating the exact patterns his parents had, as I might have in an earlier play; it felt falsely cynical. And although the statistics of abused children who grow up to be abusing parents is sadly high, I realized that in this instance Daisy's intelligence and introspection counted for me in a positive way.

I used to believe that intelligence was of little help in escaping the psychological patterns that have been inbred in one. I based this depressing belief on how overwhelming my own personal depressions were in my early twenties, and on how my mother and some other family members—smart people too—nonetheless seemed to make the same sorts of mistakes over and over in their lives, causing themselves the same kind of pain; there wasn't even *variety* in their pain. And other people I met seemed similarly stuck in repetition. So life seemed hopeless to me, and without progress.

As I left my early twenties behind, my life kept getting better, partially because I made some smart choices. I lost that sense of feeling like a child at the mercy of his parents; and though I'm not totally free of the subtle and buried kinds of psychological traps that all of us have, I found I was choosing to avoid being around or working with difficult or chaotic people. I think I'm oversensitive to tempestuous people—those for whom throwing a temper tantrum is just a way of releasing steam, but who terrify me—but by my consciously choosing to avoid those people, I did myself a great favor, I gave myself the right to protect myself. And as I felt more protected, I felt less a victim, and then happier. (Plus, there are so many talented people out there who aren't tempestuous that, indeed, why not choose someone easy and supportive over someone unpredictable and enraging?)

Anyway, I've been rather personal in analyzing why I felt more optimistic at this point in my life, but in terms of the play it was simpler. I just "knew" that Daisy would be less unpredictable to his child than his parents were to him because, through introspection and analysis, he had been so sensitized to what it had done to him; and he was smart enough to have sought help to get "better." It meant his mistakes would not be as blatant, and that actually is progress, isn't it? I had never, to my knowledge, written an ending that was "hopeful" before. And it wasn't false to me; it was what I meant, and felt. So I was excited by this ending.

Andre Bishop at Playwrights Horizons offered to do the play at his theatre in New York for November of 1983. Jerry Zaks, who had directed *Sister Mary* and the off-Broadway *Beyond Therapy,* was set to direct.

I love working with Jerry, who's extremely kind and smart, and who also loves actors, which makes them happy, which makes me happy. Jerry has gone on to become justly famous as a director, winning Obies (for my play *Marriage of Bette and Boo*) and a Tony (for his revival of John Guare's *House of Blue Leaves*), and now he's a musical director as well, having done the highly successful *Anything Goes* at Lincoln Center.

In early previews, though, something seemed wrong; the play just wasn't funny. Or one night it would be kind of funny, then the next night not at all. Some of it seemed to be the talented actress playing Helen; she was doing something other actors have also done, and which drives me crazy: she was deciding that if her character was angry on pages three, four, and eleven, she had to make sure each of these instances was "different," when they were written, more or less, to be done full throttle and to the maximum—part of what was scary, and funny, about Helen. But the actress, tied to rather old-fashioned beliefs of character "building," was wedded to using her intellect to "modulate" the character's emotions. And underneath this desire for modulation was fear: she was worried about what would happen to audience sympathy for her if she didn't do this. As you can probably tell from reading my plays, I have people fly off the handle and into rages frequently, and, frankly, in most cases, "full-out" is the best way to do these mood shifts. Anyone who's lived near someone who flies into rages knows that most of the time they fly into the 99% category, they don't run around "gradating" them.

So Jerry would direct her to be full-out, and Andre

Bishop would explain how "in Chris's plays, the characters who are really awful are the ones the audience likes
best." And she'd be better for one performance, then
slip back to doing it the way her instinct told her to.
But because she was a good actress, the effect she was
having was subtle; maybe the play was at fault, I
thought.

I then had a good actress friend come to the play. She
looked pained after the performance. She was too sensitive to just blurt out that it wasn't working, but I admit-
ted to her that something seemed wrong and I didn't
know what. I asked her if she knew, and without hesita-
tion she said, yes, you must fire the actress playing
Helen. I was shocked at her bluntness and her certainty,
but she also stilled the doubt in my mind that the fault
was in the play. Without any cues from me, this friend
"got" that the actress didn't trust the play and was
worried she'd seem unsympathetic. This worry about
sympathy, which was not explicit but just a "tone in the
air," did not belong in the world of this play; according
to my friend, if I didn't fire her, it would be the play that
would look bad, not the actress, because she was nonetheless very talented.

We did fire her the next day—or rather, Jerry did,
looking stricken and pained, but in definite agreement.
(Our unnamed friend was the epitome of caring and
honesty, and not someone to lightly suggest firing anyone, so we took her comments very seriously.)

We postponed the opening and asked Christine Estabrook to play Helen. (We had almost cast her to begin
with.) Christine was heroic and did the first two nights
holding the book, but so skillfully that one immediately forgot that she was reading. She's a fabulous
actress, extremely funny, extremely touching, and we
were lucky to have her.

The rest of the cast was a little disoriented by our

firing of the original Helen, but they all chose to let go of any doubts they had and just trust me and Jerry and get on with it. The other actors, all of whom were terrific, were W. H. Macy, Dana Ivey, Keith Reddin, and Leslie Geraci.

The play was done upstairs at Playwrights' studio theatre, which has seventy seats. Younger audiences found the play a laugh riot. As the play went on, though, the seventy seats were often filled by the Playwrights Horizons subscription audience. Subscriber audiences tend to be older, and they have agreed to come to all the plays, on a certain date, having no idea what they are to see. And they didn't like it much.

Or rather, something happened to them in Act One. They became afraid I was going to make jokes about physical abuse of infants, while, as you know from reading it, I'm just making merry about psychological abuse, which is what I know about. So some nights, the subscriber audience would not laugh once. In the entire first act. Not once. This drove the poor actors crazy. (And I didn't love it either.)

In Act Two, though, this same audience would start to laugh. And I realized it was maybe because in the first scene of Act Two, I finally had some voices of reason on the stage: Kate and Angela clearly loved their children, and were alarmed by Helen's behavior. And this gave the conservative audience a reference point; they suddenly breathed easier, and felt I wasn't actually in *favor* of child abuse.

In terms of my work, I also remembered that some of my early plays (especially *The Nature and Purpose of the Universe*) really upset some audiences because the characters' suffering was presented comically (and in great, hideous exaggeration), without there ever being a spokesperson in the play for normal decency or compassion. When I'd meet audience members who only knew my early plays, they would often express surprise that I didn't look and sound like the Wild Man of Borneo.

Looking back, I'm extremely fond of my early works that are so anarchic and horrifying; they do make me laugh, as was true for some of the audiences too. But starting with Diane's serious speech in *Sister Mary* where she straightforwardly expresses her upset with Sister and the Church, I started to drop the manic-ness from time to time and to talk seriously. And I realized that the subscriber audience at *Bathwater* missed this greatly in Act One; they felt they were trapped in a seventy-seat subway car with a lunatic.

However, luckily, we extended the run of *Bathwater* a bit, and as the subscriber audience thinned out and a more general audience came to see this *specific* play, the play fell into better balance, and we got laughs throughout again.

The reviews had been mixed—good, bad, and medium—but because *The New York Times* had been even a bit better than good, some commercial producers negotiated to move the play off-Broadway. However, the night of our last scheduled performance I learned from Andre that the deal looked 99% likely to fall through (for no particular reason, just cold feet that maybe it wasn't commercial enough, I guess). I decided to tell the actors this before the last performance so they'd know it was possible this would be their final performance. They were disappointed but took it in good stride.

For the next two years, I worked on a steamer that crossed the Atlantic from Hoboken to Burma. No, I'm kidding. I don't remember what I did. Then, in 1985, Jerry Zaks directed what I think is my best play, *The Marriage of Bette and Boo*, at the Public Theatre. (It's also published by Grove, hint, hint.) It won many Obies, and went well with the audiences, even the subscriber ones, and was, all told, pretty successful.

Sometime in late 1985, I wrote the Woman's monologue part of *Laughing Wild*. I wrote it the same way I wrote *Sister Mary*, with no particular production in mind, with no theatre, just because I had an impulse to write. I wish I always could write from that impulse.

New York City has gotten harder and harder to live in (I've been here since 1975), and part of the speech was triggered by that. Another part was triggered by choosing to let go of the "reasonableness" of my mind; I let the Woman unleash her most random complaints, and I didn't censor them or try to balance them with being fair. (Her comments on Mother Theresa are a good example; I would hardly say any of the things she says about Mother Theresa, though critics were lazily to list Mother Theresa as one of my "targets" in the play. A less lazy audience member, not trying to come up with a snappy, journalistic list of targets, told me how much she identified with the Woman's thoughts, more or less, up until the crazy comment about Mother Theresa being "just like Sally Jessy Raphael, only different," at which point she realized how deeply crazy the Woman was. The Woman's targets and mine should not be assumed to be the same.)

Early on I had a reading of the Woman's monologue, and I asked the actress-writer E. Katherine Kerr to read the part. I had been a fan of hers from having seen her at auditions (especially a hilarious interpretation of Sister Mary Ignatius), and from seeing her in Tommy Tune's production of Caryl Churchill's *Cloud 9*. Indeed, I saw her three times (and the play five times), so knocked out was I by her performance, and the play itself.

I had no idea what Katherine's presence would do to the part, but I knew she had razor-sharp comic timing and, judging from the end of *Cloud 9* in particular, an ability to be deeply (and suddenly) moving.

At this initial reading, Katherine blew the invited audience away, and I filed away in my head that I wanted to make this Woman's monologue somehow be part of a full evening.

But the project stayed on a back burner. In late 1986 I was scheduled to read from my works at the 92nd Street Y (on a bill with Wallace Shawn), and I decided to write something new in order to make use of the audience who'd be there, to test their responses. Katherine had been encouraging me to write something that I myself could act in to go with the monologue, so that's what I did. And once I had the notion that the Man was the person on the other end of the "tuna fish" story, I knew I had a good hook.

At the Y, the Man's monologue was scary to do; it felt very personal and naked. The Woman's voice was that of a character who thought and spoke very differently from myself (however much I might occasionally mirror her crazy upset). The Man's voice and concerns were much closer to my personal ones. The audience response, though, felt very electric, and I overcame my hesitations and decided that this Man's speech, reworked, should remain the companion piece to the Woman's.

The evening needed a third piece, and I kept waiting for the perfect one to spring forth from my brain. I thought of having a third character show up—maybe the street musician, or the 'cello player, or any of the other people mentioned in the Woman's speech; maybe I could make the evening be a series of character sketches, all somewhat related. But I kept feeling that having the Man and the Woman interact would be the most satisfying and logical premise for the third piece. But *how* to have them interact, in a real or even semi-real situation, stumped me. Their history of attack and illogic in the supermarket seemed to offer little opening for conversation that I could figure out.

Then I thought of having them dream about one another, and of the (I hoped) theatrical effect of having their dreams (and obsessions) intersect with one another.

I also felt that the third piece—and the evening as a whole—should be written intuitively and be less reasoned out. And I guess I think I failed in this—my intuitive glands are just too blocked still. The third piece is rather *willfully* intuitive.

Having been, I hope, disarmingly honest about this, still I think plays are rarely perfect, and there are chunks of the third piece that do work. The opening re-enactment of the supermarket event, done in various versions, worked very well indeed. Their spoken dreams are okay, and do serve the function of explaining how their dreams are overlapping with one another. The Infant of Prague sequence is (or was) much fun for the audience (and for me to perform), but its sketch energy probably pulls us away from a clear connection to the genuine psyches of the Woman and the Man.

Then, at the Harmonic Convergence, I feel the dream is on to something thematically compelling and resonant. And some audience members told me they felt very complete with the play and its ending. And some audience members (and most critics in their reviews) found the ending unbelievably hopeful (and sappy), and just totally unengaging.

I don't know what I think. Or rather, I think several things, some of them contradictory.

Preview audiences seemed to love the entire evening,

and to be *really really* engaged. The invited audience
the night *before* the critics and the night *after* the
critics was ecstatic. (Invited houses are, of course,
geared to like it, yet I don't have enough friends to
explain when an audience response is *ecstatic.*) The
night the critics attended was weird and unpleasant.
Being in a play where both characters talk *to* the audience, and having to talk to this particular group of
people, especially in a small theatre, where their presence predominates—well, it was difficult. The energy
of the critics is very different from a normal house.
They've come to *judge:* that's what their job is, and how
most of them view it. It's hard not to become self-
conscious in that atmosphere. Remember when you
were a child, and a teacher or a parent put you under
scrutiny and said grimly: Okay, now let's see what you
can do. You invariably freeze. You wouldn't freeze in
front of a *nurturing* parent or teacher, but in front of a
judgmental one, it's pretty hard not to. That's what
theatre performers are up against during critics' nights:
a strange, judgmental, cerebral atmosphere that is *nothing* like performing for a regular audience. Oh well, I'm
off on critics again. Give it a rest, Chris.

Then after the reviews and previews, we were back off
on the subscription houses again. And they liked this
better than *Baby with the Bathwater*—they actually
agreed with the Woman's sense of rage and upset, and
they grew to like the Man. (The actor in me, I sometimes feared, made him more ingratiating than he
maybe should have been, in order to make some of his
opinions on sexuality more palatable to the fairly con-
ventional audience.)

But I found the run very stressful.

I usually enjoy performing—and I had greatly enjoyed being in *The Marriage of Bette and Boo*—but

performing in *Laughing Wild* ended up being harder, and more complicated, for me.

The Man's monologue is very personal, and I'm a mixture of introvert and extrovert. Some days I'd be at the theatre and not *want* to get up in front of the audience and express myself so nakedly. But then for that thirty minute monologue, I would have to *pretend* to be outgoing. Of course, that's what acting is, pretending; but these monologues felt as if they should be genuinely felt, not just performed; and when I would feel reclusive and not communicative, it felt very uncomfortable to do this play. (I also probably internalized a lot of the critics' judgments, which also made me want to withdraw and not be outgoing.)

And then here I was again with the subscriber audiences. As I said, they liked it (and sometimes told us so), but they were hard to play to; the previews had gotten us used to being rewarded by *big* laughs, and now, though we still got laughs, it felt as if we were pulling the audience along with us. (I remember after one matinee, Katherine and I were having lunch, bemoaning how quiet and nonresponsive the house had been, when four women in their late sixties came over and told us how much they had just *loved* the play and how it made them think and so on. This was a big boost, so we got better at deciding that a quieter house didn't necessarily mean they were disinterested. Indeed, Katherine pointed out that the loudly laughing audiences were probably made up of people who already saw the world in the terms the play did, and that maybe the quieter houses "needed" to be exposed to the play's viewpoint more than our demonstrative houses did. Sometimes that gave me a sense of purpose: there were audiences that needed to be exposed to this play. Other times my sense of purpose would drop down to zero, and I would await going to hell in a handbasket with everyone else in New York City.)

Our last week (which no one knew was our last week due to confusing publicity from Playwrights), the subscribers were over, and we had only audiences who came to see the specific show. And all eight performances were glorious, as the invited previews had been; but these audiences weren't invited, they were just whoever came and paid that night. It made me feel the play and the performance *were* a success. I wish we had run longer so I could have had more of that, to convince me the play was successful with audiences, or at least to test whether those performances were just flukes. But having the last eight in a row be so well received was at least a nice note on which to finish up.

I got to do the Man's monologue on its own this past summer at the Theatre Communications Group conference in Northampton, Massachusetts. TCG is the organization of all the regional theatres, and so the audience at this conference was of theatre professionals from all over the country. I loved performing it there, knowing I wasn't going to be reviewed; audience response would be my one and only critique. And I was thrilled with the TCG audience's response. Audiences want to be entertained, and they also want to be engaged in issues that are important to them. This one-time performance helped me feel better about the writing in *Laughing Wild.* The electricity between the piece, me, and the audience seemed so evident to me that I simply don't understand the blankness with which it was received critically in New York.

I sound like a stuck record about critics, so what topic can I end on that doesn't concern them?

I keep meaning to talk about the "New Age" stuff in *Laughing Wild.* The Man clearly dabbles in it, without its really working for him, and that's true of me as well as him. Probably one of the sincerest lines in the monologue, for me, is, "I'm *starved* for some meaning . . . I'm tired of being an existentialist." Maybe it's my Catholic religious upbringing, which instilled in me as a child the belief in a Father God with intricate, involved plans for your life; with its guardian angels (like ethereal teddy bears) floating around, trying to guide you in the right direction; with its myriad of saints with special skills (like St. Anthony for finding lost things, and, most appropriate for the 20th century, St. Jude for magical help in hopeless causes).

The New Age is kind of like secular humanism married to a sense of magic: crystals and the earth and our own bodies have healing properties that we have forgotten about; there are spirit guides floating around, with advice and solace and direction; if there isn't a great big Father up there to guide and judge (and condemn) us, there's a belief in a God within that we are all a part of. The world and its chaos seem so far outside our control, it's very attractive to believe or at least entertain belief in these sorts of things in order to more easily walk around, putting one foot after another. And because I do believe in intuition—which is a nonlinear kind of knowing—there is a part of me perfectly willing to think there's a whole litany of different kinds of knowledge that humankind could have access to.

So some days I'm a sort of semi-believer.

And then other days, alas, I switch back to finding life an enormous, meaningless effort. And on those days I try not to talk on the telephone, and I sit in a chair and meditate on Peggy Lee singing "Is That All There Is?" And I wait for feelings of optimism to return.